DAY OF GLORY

The Life of Bahá'u'lláh

DAY OF GLORY

The Life of Bahá'u'lláh

by

Mary Perkins

Illustrated

by

Susan Reed

GR

GEORGE RONALD

OXFORD

GEORGE RONALD, Publisher
46 High Street, Kidlington, Oxford OX5 2DN

British Library Cataloguing in Publication Data

Perkins, Mary
Day of glory: the life of Baha'u'llah.
I. Title
297.93

ISBN 0–85398–347–X
ISBN 0–85398–339–9 Pbk

CONTENTS

This book is dedicated
to the Bahá'ís of Írán, past and present,
men and women, youth and children,
in token of an immeasurable debt

I, Myself, am but the first servant,
to believe in Him and in His signs.[1]

The Báb

If on the day of His Revelation
all that are on earth
bear Him allegiance,
Mine inmost being will rejoice,
inasmuch as all will have attained
the summit of their existence.[2]

The Báb

PREFACE

READERS of *Hour of the Dawn* will already be familiar with the main events of the Báb's life. This volume, *Day of Glory*, begins in 1817 with the birth of Bahá'u'lláh. The Báb was born in 1819.

Chapters 2, 3 and 4 cover the years of the Báb's mission, 1844–1850. A certain overlap in narrative in both volumes is unavoidable. This time the focus is on the many ways that Bahá'u'lláh served the Cause of the Báb during those tumultuous years.

Marzieh Gail reminds us in *The Sheltering Branch* that:

> At a certain point in time two thousand years ago there was only one pivotal fact in the world: the life of Christ. And the nineteenth century, in its turn, saw only one pivotal fact: intertwined lives of the Báb and Bahá'u'lláh . . .[1]

In Chapter 4 the thread of narrative which was broken at the end of *Hour of the Dawn* is regained. The siege of Zanján began in May 1850, two months before the Báb laid down his life for Bahá'u'lláh, of whom He had earlier written:

> If on the day of His Revelation all that are on earth bear Him allegiance, Mine inmost being will rejoice, inasmuch as all will have attained the summit of their existence.[2]

Bahá'u'lláh's House in Ṭihrán where He was born.

CHAPTER 1

EARLY YEARS

ṬIHRÁN, the capital city of Persia, lies in a saucer-shaped hollow at the foot of the southern slopes of the Alburz mountains. The great hills form an encircling backdrop to the city; to the north-east the snow-capped, cone-shaped peak of Mount Damávand stands sentinel, to the south the vast empty desert of central Persia laps its dusty waves at the very feet of the city.

Nightfall and daybreak come with swiftness here. On clear winter mornings the sun leaps from behind the northern slopes of Damávand and suddenly, brilliantly, it is day. The long-drawn, resonant invocations of the call to prayer rise from the city's mosques and resound through the waking streets, summoning the faithful Muslims to their morning prayers.

Between dawn and sunrise on 12 November 1817 a child was born in Ṭihrán to a nobleman of Núr, Mírzá 'Abbás, known as Mírzá Buzurg, the Vizier, and his second wife, a lady of noble birth named Khadíjih Khánum. The child was born in the large town house near the Shimrán Gate at the eastern edge of the city where Mírzá Buzurg and his family spent each winter. On that November dawn the family and the entire large household gave joyful, grateful thanks for the safe delivery of a son and for the good health of Khadíjih Khánum, His mother. His parents, who already had a daughter and a son, named their third child Ḥusayn 'Alí. He is known to us by a name given to Him by the Báb. It is 'Bahá'u'lláh' and it means 'the Light, Glory and Splendour of God'.

Few children born in Persia or anywhere else in the world of 1817 were as fortunate as the Vizier's son. K͟hadíjih K͟hánum was a devoted wife and mother and the children of the Vizier were heirs to riches and noble rank. They were accustomed, from earliest childhood, to every comfort and elegance of living and every refinement of culture that Persia in 1817 could offer them. Moreover, the Vizier was an upright and honourable man who occupied a high office of state and was held in great esteem by his sovereign and his countrymen. His considerable learning and superb calligraphic skills had brought him wide renown. His marked sense of justice and his compassion for others less fortunate than himself set him apart from the flattery and self-seeking of the royal court.

Already a widow when she married the Vizier, K͟hadíjih K͟hánum had three children from her first marriage while Mírzá Buzurg had two sons from his first marriage. This latest child, Mírzá Ḥusayn 'Alí, astonished both His parents. He never cried nor was He restless and fretful like their other children. He was always alert, quiet and contented. Mírzá Buzurg paid very little attention to the rest of his children but he quickly became devoted to Bahá'u'lláh.

One day when Bahá'u'lláh was seven years old both His parents were watching Him as He walked nearby. His mother remarked that He was a little short in stature but His father replied:

'It is of no importance. Are you not aware of His capacity and His abilities? Such intelligence! And such perception! He is as a flame of fire. Even at this young age He surpasses mature men.'[1]

Once, when Bahá'u'lláh was still only seven years old, one of Fatḥ-'Alí S͟háh's tax collectors unjustly demanded from Mírzá Buzurg a large sum of money. The Vizier had already paid all the taxes that he owed but the grasping official compelled him to pay again. Emboldened by this success and aware that Mírzá Buzurg was a man of great wealth, he made a second and then a third, even larger demand. Bahá'u'lláh could not tolerate such injustice. He set out on a two-day journey to reach the Sháh. Once in the royal presence He pleaded His father's case so ably and with such eloquence that the Sháh dismissed his dishonest tax collector.

The male children of the Persian nobility were tutored privately at their homes and their education was strictly limited. They learnt how to ride and hunt, how to handle guns and swords and they were taught the elaborate, courtly manners of their class. They learnt the basic skills of calligraphy, some classical Persian poetry and were taught to read the Qur'án. It was soon widely rumoured that the Vizier's son had no need of a tutor. Untaught, He could answer any difficult question put to Him and He happily plunged into discussions of subjects which were considered the exclusive domain of men who had studied theology, philosophy and religious law.

'The learning current amongst men I studied not,' Bahá'u'lláh later wrote in a letter to Náṣiri'd-Dín Sháh, 'their schools I entered not. Ask of the city wherein I dwelt, that thou mayest be well assured that I am not of them who speak falsely.'[2]

His remarkable intellectual powers, His wisdom and extraordinary intelligence astonished relatives, strangers and friends alike. His wide-ranging knowledge, His unequalled mastery of argument and eloquence of speech were not barriers separating Him from others for they were matched by great charm, humility and sweetness of spirit. Bahá'u'lláh's warm heart and the delight He took in people, His lively sense of humour, and His patient, generous nature endeared Him to all and drew to Him people of all classes and ages.

In the summer months the wealthy inhabitants of Ṭihrán fled the heat and disease-ridden dust of the capital for their country estates in the provinces or for their summer residences on the slopes above the city. The Vizier had a house in Shimrán, a village on a wooded slope just above Ṭihrán but as he and his wife came from the province of Mázindarán, they would move there whenever possible.

Mázindarán lies between the curving southern shore of the Caspian Sea and the Alburz mountains. For centuries the poets of Persia have written in praise of this warm, temperate land of orchards, forests and streams, of the deer in its woods, the hawks soaring in its skies, the fish in its clear streams and the hyacinths and tulips that fill its meadows with fragrance and colour. In Mázindarán, it is said, the roses bloom and the nightingales sing in every season of the year.

The contrast between the moist forested slopes and fertile plains of Mázindarán and the dry plateau where Ṭihrán is situated is extreme. A traveller in our own century, Robert Byron, on reaching the pass which leads over the edge of the central plateau and down to the Caspian coast, described the change in these words:

> In five minutes we had escaped from a world of stone and mud and sand and everlasting drought into one of wood and leaves and moisture, where the hills were clothed with bushes, the bushes grew into trees, and the trees gathered into a glowing forest . . . The oppression of the plateau was suddenly remitted . . . the relief was actually physical. Our bodies seemed to undergo a change of gravity, a return of normal buoyancy.[3]

Mírzá Buzurg was a member of one of the most ancient and distinguished families of Mázindarán. He was descended from Zoroaster, the Messenger of God Who appeared in Persia over two thousand years ago. He was also a descendant of Yazdigird III, the last king of the Sásánian dynasty which ruled Persia for eight hundred years before the Muslim conquest. Khadíjih Khánum was descended from Abraham and his wife Keturah.

Mírzá Buzurg chose a site in his ancestral village of Tákur and there he built a stately mansion. He employed skilled craftsmen and artists to decorate and embellish it and he furnished it with the finest carpets and precious works of art. Bahá'u'lláh spent part of every year in Tákur and many hours and days roaming the orchards and meadows of Núr. He developed, at an early age, a deep and enduring love of the natural world. He far preferred the countryside to the city and had no interest in spending time at the royal court. Instead, He spent His days in helping the poor and oppressed, giving food, shelter, comfort and advice to all who came to Him in need.

In October 1835, when Bahá'u'lláh was nearly eighteen, He married Ásíyih Khánum, the daughter of a noble family of Yálrúd, in Mázindarán. Ásíyih Khánum, to whom Bahá'u'lláh gave the title Navváb, was a tall, slender and graceful girl with vivid, dark-blue eyes. She was vivacious and tender-hearted, wise beyond her years and full of compassion for others. Both Bahá'u'lláh and Ásíyih Khánum inherited large fortunes from their parents. Ásíyih Khánum's family hired a jeweller especially to make the jewels for her dowry and the work took six months; even the buttons on her dresses were of gold set with precious jewels. When she left her father's home for the home of her husband, forty mules were needed to transport all her possessions. However, Ásíyih Khánum shared Bahá'u'lláh's distaste for ostentation and luxurious living and she too preferred to live in the country rather than at court.

At that time, only a few people in Persia enjoyed great wealth and the majority of the population lived in poverty and want. Wherever they were, whether in Ṭihrán or

Mázindarán, Bahá'u'lláh and Ásíyih Khánum opened their doors to the hungry and troubled. Amongst the poorer classes they became known as 'Father of the Poor' and 'Mother of Consolation'. They soon had their own share of grief for the first two children born to them both died in infancy.

In those years there was a most learned and highly respected mujtahid named Mírzá Muḥammad Taqí living in Núr. One day, while the mujtahid was speaking to over two hundred of his students, Bahá'u'lláh passed that way with a small group of His friends. They paused for a while to listen. The mujtahid was asking his disciples to explain the meaning of an obscure passage in a certain hadíth, an Islamic spoken tradition. When all the students admitted that they were unable to give an explanation, Bahá'u'lláh spoke. He gave a brief but lucid and convincing explanation of the tradition in question. The mujtahid scolded his own students.

'For years', he exclaimed, 'I have been instructing you and have patiently striven to instil into your minds the profoundest truths and the noblest principles of the Faith. And yet you allow, after all these years of persistent study, this youth . . . who has had no share in scholarly training, and who is entirely unfamiliar with your academic learning, to demonstrate his superiority over you!'[4]

When Bahá'u'lláh left the gathering, the mujtahid related to his disciples that he had recently had two unusual dreams. 'In my first dream,' he recounted, 'I was standing in the midst of a vast concourse of people, all of whom seemed to be pointing to a certain house in which they said the Ṣáḥibu'z-Zamán [the Lord of the Age] dwelt. Frantic with joy, I hastened in my dream to attain His presence. When I reached the house, I was, to my great surprise, refused admittance. "The promised Qá'im", I was informed, "is engaged in private conversation with another Person. Access to them is strictly forbidden." From the guards who were standing beside the door, I gathered that that Person was none other than Bahá'u'lláh.

'In my second dream,' the mujtahid continued, 'I found myself in a place where I beheld around me a number of coffers, each of which, it was stated, belonged to Bahá'u-'lláh. As I opened them, I found them to be filled with books. Every word and letter recorded in these books was set with the most exquisite jewels. Their radiance dazzled me. I was so overpowered by their brilliance that I awoke suddenly from my dream.'[5]

Between 1810 and 1830, Bahá'u'lláh's father, Mírzá Buzurg, enjoyed two decades of remarkable prosperity but in the early 1830s a series of calamities fell upon him. First of all, a great flood of exceptional violence swept down from the mountains of Mázindarán and through the village of Tákur. The floodwater utterly demolished one half of the Vizier's palatial mansion, swept away or smashed the costly furniture and irretrievably ruined the carpets and the elaborate ornamentation of the house. Next, Mírzá Buzurg incurred the anger of Ḥájí Mírzá Áqásí, the newly-appointed Grand Vizier.

Mírzá Buzurg was a close friend of the distinguished Mírzá Abu'l-Qásim, Qá'im-Maqám, who had held the post of Grand Vizier at the court of Fatḥ-'Alí Sháh. Both men kept themselves apart from the gossip, intrigue, rivalry and cruelty that centred on the royal court. In 1834, when Fatḥ-'Alí Sháh died, Qá'im-Maqám was instrumental in ensuring that Muḥammad Sháh, a grandson of the late Sháh, succeeded to the throne. The new Sháh repaid his debt to his gifted and honourable minister by promptly arranging for his murder.

Mírzá Buzurg was appalled. He strongly suspected that the sudden fall from power and cruel death of Qá'im Maqám had been engineered by the new Grand Vizier, Ḥájí Mírzá

Áqásí, the former tutor of the new Sháh. Outraged and grieving for his friend, he was unable to remain silent. A letter in which he expressed his horror and disgust at this murder fell into the hands of Ḥájí Mírzá Áqásí himself.

The incensed Grand Vizier retaliated quickly. Mírzá Buzurg's personal prestige, his great wealth, noble ancestry and the exalted station to which Fatḥ-'Alí Sháh had raised him could not save him from the vengeful wrath of the new Grand Vizier. Ḥájí Mírzá Áqásí arranged for Mírzá Buzurg to be dismissed from the governorship of Burújird and Luristán even though the Vizier's services in that post had earned him the written praise and commendation of the Sháh. He also stopped payment of an annual allowance Mírzá Buzurg was paid by the government. Mírzá Buzurg was obliged to sell a number of his properties, including the complex of houses near the Shimrán Gate where he and his family lived, and to mortgage others.

Through all the troubles that had burst so precipitately upon him, Mírzá Buzurg retained his dignity and serenity. He continued, within the means left to him, the charitable acts of earlier and more prosperous days. He made plans to retire to 'Iráq and to end his days near the holy shrines of Karbilá but he died in Ṭihrán in 1839. His body was carried to 'Iráq and was buried in Najaf.

Before His father's death Bahá'u'lláh had assumed responsibility for all but one of his younger brothers and step-brothers and for most of his father's dependents. He rented back the house near the Shimrán Gate from its new owner and lived there quietly with His family and relatives. Although Ḥájí Mírzá Áqásí had ruined Mírzá Buzurg's career and destroyed his domestic tranquillity, the new Grand Vizier greatly admired Bahá'u'lláh and often actively sought His company. Bahá'u'lláh was courteous in return but He did nothing to encourage this friendship and sought no favours. After His father's death it was widely assumed in court circles that Bahá'u'lláh would soon seek a political appointment but it is related that the Grand Vizier himself dismissed these rumours. Bahá'u'lláh, he is reported to have said, was intended for a work of far greater magnitude. The arena of government was, he is said to have observed, too small a field for His capacities. Very soon, however, Bahá'u'lláh, like His father before Him, incurred the wrath of Ḥájí Mírzá Áqásí.

Ḥájí Mírzá Áqásí was seized with a sudden desire to own a village which belonged to Bahá'u'lláh and a number of other people. Instead of asking all the owners involved if they would sell their property, the Grand Vizier tried to obtain possession of the village by fraudulent means. As soon as He learnt of this, Bahá'u'lláh, with the consent of all the other owners, sold the property to a sister of Muḥammad Sháh who had long wanted to purchase it. Thwarted, Ḥájí Mírzá Aqásí then tried to forcibly seize the property. When that failed, he referred the case to Muḥammad Sháh who ordered his minister to give up his flimsy claim to ownership. Balked again, Ḥájí Mírzá Áqásí angrily summoned Bahá'u'lláh to his presence, roundly abused Him and tried by every means in his power to discredit Him. Bahá'u'lláh vigorously defended His own actions and proved to all present His own innocence. Ḥájí Mírzá Áqásí then accused Bahá'u'lláh of plotting against him. Bahá'u'lláh again ably defended Himself and established His complete innocence. His prestige in court circles rose even higher as a result of this incident but that fact was of no interest or importance to Him.

When the Báb declared His mission to Mullá Ḥusayn in Shíráz in May of 1844, Bahá'u'lláh was living quietly in Ṭihrán. In August of the same year Mullá Ḥusayn reached Ṭihrán charged with a mysterious and 'unspeakably glorious' mission.

'A secret lies hidden in that city,' the Báb had confided to him. 'When made manifest, it shall turn the earth into paradise. My hope is that you may partake of its grace and recognize its splendour.'[6]

The Báb gave Mullá Ḥusayn a scroll written in His own hand and told him to take it to Ṭihrán. He did not tell him who the letter was intended for but advised him to pray and meditate and to search in the capital. He would know, the Báb assured Mullá Ḥusayn, as soon as he discovered the person for whom the scroll was intended.

Mullá Ḥusayn, obedient to the Báb's instructions, travelled to Ṭihrán and rented a simple room in a theological college near the Shimrán Gate. There he met with a young theological student named Mullá Muḥammad whose home was in Núr. From him Mullá Ḥusayn learnt of the distinguished and brilliant son of the late Mírzá Buzurg Who cheered the disconsolate and fed the hungry, Who had no rank or position at court but Who befriended the poor and the stranger, Who delighted in the beauty of the countryside. Mullá Ḥusayn knew that his search in Ṭihrán was over. With joy and wonder he handed to Mullá Muḥammad the scroll which the Báb had entrusted to him and asked him to deliver it to Bahá'u'lláh early the next day.

At daybreak, Mullá Muḥammad approached the house near the Shimrán Gate and there met with Mírzá Músá, the brother of Bahá'u'lláh. When he had explained the purpose of his visit, he waited as Mírzá Músá went into the house. He soon returned and invited Mullá Muḥammad to enter. Once inside, Mullá Muḥammad presented the scroll to Mírzá Músá who laid it before Bahá'u'lláh. Bahá'u'lláh picked it up, unrolled it, glanced at its contents and then began to read aloud certain of its passages. When He had read just one page of the scroll, He turned to His brother and said: 'Músá, what have you to say? Verily I say, whoso believes in the Qur'án and recognizes its Divine origin, and yet hesitates, though it be for a moment, to admit that these soul-stirring words are endowed with the same regenerating power, has most assuredly erred in his judgement and has strayed far from the path of justice.'[7]

With these words Bahá'u'lláh put Himself on the side of a new and unknown movement. From that moment, He devoted all His energy and His exceptional talents to spreading this new message of joy and hope amongst His countrymen and women. Whatever risks He had taken so far in standing up to the greed and tyranny of Ḥájí Mírzá Áqásí were trifling in comparison with the dangers that now lay ahead of Him.

CHAPTER 2

AN EXEMPLARY DISCIPLE

'O MY beloved friends! . . . Scatter throughout the length and breadth of this land, and, with steadfast feet and sanctified hearts, prepare the way for His coming.'[1] With these words the Báb sent out his first disciples, the Letters of the Living, to teach His Cause.

As soon as Bahá'u'lláh became a follower of the Báb, He travelled to His own home district of Núr in order to share the good news of the coming of the Báb with His own people. As soon as He arrived in Núr, many of the distinguished citizens of the area came to welcome Him. They eagerly asked for the latest news from the capital and the court. Bahá'u'lláh had little to tell them of the court but He spoke eloquently of the Báb's message and of the inestimable benefits it would bring to their country. His noble relatives, His friends and acquaintances were all amazed that a person of His background, rank and age should interest Himself in some new and obscure religious movement. These were matters, they considered, best left to the bearded divines and learned theologians.

Undeterred by indifference or scorn, Bahá'u'lláh continued on His chosen course. Refreshed and invigorated by the new teachings, He radiated a joyous confidence. The dignity and purity of His life, His humility, His magnetic eloquence, His incisive intellectual abilities and unanswerable logic stirred the souls of the people of Núr and led many of them to investigate the Cause of the Báb.

One of Bahá'u'lláh's uncles, alarmed at the teachings his nephew was promoting, appealed to the new mujtahid of

Núr, Mullá Muḥammad, the son of the erudite and lately deceased Mírza Muḥammad-Taqí, for assistance.

'O vicegerent of the Prophet of God!' he said. 'Behold what has befallen the Faith. A youth, a layman, attired in the garb of nobility, has come to Núr, has invaded the strongholds of orthodoxy, and disrupted the holy Faith of Islám. Arise, and resist his onslaught. Whoever attains his presence falls immediately under his spell, and is enthralled by the power of his utterance . . '[2]

Mullá Muḥammad, feeling himself quite unequal to this task, returned an evasive answer. His students, however, were not satisfied with this response. At their insistence Mullá Muḥammad appointed two of his most able students, Mullá 'Abbás and Mírzá Abu'l-Qásim, both trusted disciples of his late father, to visit Bahá'u'lláh and to determine the truth of the matter. He solemnly pledged that he would accept whatever conclusions they arrived at without qualification or reserve.

When the mujtahid's emissaries reached Bahá'u'lláh's presence, He was giving to a group of seekers an explanation of the opening súrih of the Qur'án. The loftiness of His theme and His singular eloquence deeply impressed them both. Mullá 'Abbás arose from his seat, retreated to the entrance of the room and stood there in an attitude of reverent submissiveness.

'You behold my condition,' he said to Mírzá Abu'l-Qásim. 'I am powerless to question Bahá'u'lláh. The questions I had planned to ask Him have vanished suddenly from my memory. You are free either to proceed with your enquiry or to return alone to our teacher and inform him of the state in which I find myself. Tell him from me that 'Abbás can never again return to him. He can no longer forsake this threshold.'

His companion replied, 'I have ceased to recognize my teacher. This very moment, I have vowed to God to dedicate the remaining days of my life to the service of Bahá'u'lláh, my true and only Master.'[3]

Mullá Muḥammad broke the pledge he had made to accept the verdict of his emissaries but the news of their meeting with Bahá'u'lláh and of their decision to serve Him aroused considerable interest. News of Bahá'u'lláh's activities in Núr reached Mullá Ḥusayn in Khurásán and in a letter to the Báb, he wrote an account of the events that had taken place in Ṭihrán and of Bahá'u'lláh's activities in Mázindarán. The only companion of the Báb, on the night that letter reached Him, was Quddús, with whom He shared a number of its passages. The Báb's maternal uncle later recounted: 'That night I saw such evidences of joy and gladness on the faces of the Báb and of Quddús as I am unable to describe. I often heard the Báb in those days, exultingly repeat the words, "How marvellous, how exceedingly marvellous, is that which has occurred between the months of Jamádí and Rajab!"'[4]

It was only after this letter from Mullá Ḥusayn was received that the Báb began to make the necessary preparations for his intended pilgrimage to Mecca.

One day, while out riding with His companions in Núr, Bahá'u'lláh came upon a lonely youth, a dervish, by the roadside. The dervish had made a fire and was cooking his food.

'Tell Me, dervish,' Bahá'u'lláh asked gently, 'what is it that you are doing?'

'I am engaged in eating God,' he bluntly replied. 'I am cooking God and am burning Him.'

This simple, candid reply pleased Bahá'u'lláh. He began to speak with the youth and in a short time, with great tenderness, enlightened him as to the true nature of God. Leaving behind his cooking utensils, the dervish followed on foot behind Bahá'u'lláh, composing and chanting love-songs to the One who had brought new understanding to his heart.

'Thou art the Day-Star of guidance,' he sang repeatedly. 'Thou art the Light of Truth. Unveil Thyself to men, O Revealer of the Truth.'[5]

Once back in Ṭihrán Bahá'u'lláh continued to champion, vigorously and fearlessly, the Cause of the Báb. Such action carried considerable risk. In Shíráz, Quddús and two other Bábís had been savagely beaten, their beards had been burnt, their noses pierced and they had been led through the city on halters and expelled from it, their execution threatened if they dared to return. In 'Iráq, Mullá 'Alí, boldly proclaiming the Báb's message in Karbilá and Najaf, had encountered the full fury of the divines. He was in prison in Baghdád. Wherever the Bábís spoke out, they risked their lives. However, Bahá'u'lláh's personal prestige and considerable wealth enabled Him to shelter and assist the less privileged believers. His home became a focal point for the small Bábí community of the city and a magnet to those who were obliged to travel through the capital.

In 1847 the Báb was a guest in the home of Manúchihr Khán, the Governor of Iṣfahán. But on the Governor's death, the Báb's presence in his house was discovered and He was summoned by the Sháh to Ṭihrán. When the Báb was only twenty-eight miles away from the capital, the Grand Vizier, desperate to prevent the Sháh from meeting the Báb, had the little cavalcade diverted to Kulayn, a village that he owned. When word reached Ṭihrán that the Báb was lodged at Kulayn, Bahá'u'lláh sent a small group of Bábís to Kulayn with gifts and a sealed letter for the Báb. The Báb received them delightedly and the sadness which had weighed on His soul ever since leaving Shíráz lifted from Him. Joy and exultation shone from His face.

One early dawn the Báb's guards were alarmed to discover that He was not in His tent. They searched frantically for Him and found Him walking alone towards them from the direction of Ṭihrán. So overawed were they by the serene majesty of His bearing and the radiance of His countenance that they were unable to say a word to Him. One of the Bábís present on that morning later recounted: 'A look of confidence had settled upon His countenance, His words were invested with such transcendent power, that a feeling of profound reverence wrapped our very souls. No one dared to question Him as to the cause of so remarkable a change in His speech and demeanour. Nor did He Himself choose to allay our curiosity and wonder.'[6]

When Mullá Ḥusayn walked from Mashhad to Máh-Kú and back again in order to visit the Báb, it was Bahá'u'lláh's house in Ṭihrán that he visited both on his way and on returning. When Ḥájí Mullá Taqí, Ṭáhirih's uncle, was murdered in Qazvín and Ṭáhirih was put under house arrest, it was Bahá'u'lláh who swiftly took action. He sent a trusted friend, a man who wielded considerable influence at court, to the Grand Vizier to explain the facts of the situation and establish the innocence of the Bábís. Once assured that this information had been well received, Bahá'u'lláh went to visit the Bábís from Qazvín who were held captive in Ṭihrán. He gave money to the prison officials for the purchase of food and clothes for the prisoners. The murderer of Ḥají Mullá Taqí soon confessed to his crime, but, finding that no one was interested in his confession – the murdered man's relatives were much too busy trying to blame his death on the Bábís – he escaped from prison.

The relatives of the murdered mullá then rushed from Qazvín to Ṭihrán where they accused Bahá'u'lláh of helping the murderer to escape. Fully aware of these accusations, Bahá'u'lláh went again to visit the Bábí prisoners. He was arrested and kept in confinement for several days, until His friends at court intervened on His behalf and proved that the accusations were baseless. One of the imprisoned Bábís was executed in Ṭihrán and the others were sent back to Qazvín.

The divines of the town and the aggrieved relatives whipped the populace into a frenzy of rage against the Bábís. On their arrival at Qazvín, a bloodthirsty mob fell upon the Bábí prisoners. Armed with knives, swords, spears, hatchets and axes, they hacked the defenceless men to pieces. No one in Qazvín protested.

The jubilant relatives of Ḥájí Mullá Taqí now determined to put Ṭáhirih to death. Bahá'u'lláh quickly sent a young Bábí who had fled from the town at the start of the troubles back to Qazvín to rescue her. Risking his own life by returning to his home town, but following exactly the precise instructions given to him by Bahá'u'lláh, he escorted Ṭáhirih out of Qazvín from under the very noses of her gaolers. Her sudden and unaccountable disappearance threw the whole town into uproar. A watch was set for her at the town gates but by that time she and her rescuer had already left and were travelling swiftly along an unfrequented route to Ṭihrán. Before the next daybreak she was safely in Bahá'u'lláh's house. A watch was even set for her at all the gates of Ṭihrán but Bahá'u'lláh arranged for her to leave, unnoticed, through the eastern gate for Khurásán.

When the Báb, imprisoned in Chihríq, directed His followers to assemble in Mázindarán, it was Bahá'u'lláh Who hosted the meeting of the Bábís at Badasht and it was His unobtrusive leadership that enabled them to make a decisive break with the laws and observances of Islám. At Níyálá, just after the conference, when they were attacked by about five hundred angry villagers, it was Bahá'u'lláh, almost alone in the general panic, Who stood His ground, shielded Quddús from a savage attack and helped him to safety, ensured the safety of Ṭáhirih and, once the violence of the attack was over, managed to recover part of the Bábís' plundered property. Having arranged for Ṭáhirih to be escorted out of the area, He went on His way towards Núr.

Rumours of a gathering of Bábís in Mázindarán had

reached Ṭihrán and a number of courtiers, jealous of Bahá'u'lláh's prestige at court, reported to Muḥammad Sháh that He was instigating a rebellion in the province. Though the Sháh was at first unwilling to listen to their reports, they eventually succeeded in poisoning his mind against Bahá'u'lláh.

'I have hitherto', the Sháh stormed, 'refused to countenance whatever has been said against him. My indulgence has been actuated by my recognition of the services rendered to my country by his father. This time, however, I am determined to put him to death.'[7]

An order promptly went out for the arrest of Bahá'u'lláh. He was to be brought to Ṭihrán without delay. Bahá'u'lláh was at this time travelling by easy stages to Núr and the royal edict reached Him at Bandar-jaz, a port on the Caspian Sea. Several notables of the town and the Russian agent at the port urged Him to leave the country at once in a Russian ship that was docked there. He gently refused this advice.

A banquet was to be held the next day in His honour and many men of prominence from the area had been invited especially to meet Him. Just before the banquet began a courier galloped into Bandar-Jaz with momentous news. Breathless from a headlong ride, he gave his news – Muḥammad Sháh was dead. The royal edict ordering Bahá'u'lláh's arrest no longer carried any authority. Ḥájí Mírzá Áqasí's influence and authority were also at an end. A new ruler, Náṣiri'd-Dín Sháh, succeeded to the throne and a new Grand Vizier, Mírzá Taqí Khán, was appointed.

In the meantime, both Ṭáhirih and Quddús had been arrested. Quddús was thrown into prison in Ámul, the capital of Mázindarán. Ṭáhirih was taken to Ṭihrán and placed under house arrest in the home of the Kalántar, or mayor, of the city.

CHAPTER 3

A DARKENING LAND

In the summer of 1848 the persecution of the Bábís intensified and a veritable whirlwind of calamity overtook the infant Faith. These calamities were triggered by the startling claim made by the Báb in Tabríz that summer. Summoned by the Grand Vizier from His prison cell at Chihríq to appear and face chastisement before a convocation of the nation's religious leaders, the Báb was asked Whom He claimed to be and what message He brought.

'I am, I am, I am the promised One!' the Báb replied. 'I am the One whose name you have for a thousand years invoked, at whose mention you have risen, whose advent you have longed to witness, and the hour of whose Revelation you have prayed God to hasten.'[1]

This clear and bold declaration galvanized the energies of both His followers and His enemies. It provoked a nationwide, heated controversy which reverberated through crowded bazaars and dusty village squares. The powers of church and state, fearful of losing their hold on the population, joined hands in instigating a fierce and systematic campaign of persecution designed to exterminate the Bábí community and to extinguish the light of hope which the Báb had kindled in His darkened homeland.

Mullá Ḥusayn, released from a detention that had prevented him attending the conference at Badasht, was preparing to leave Mashhad for Karbilá when a letter from the Báb reached him, requesting him to raise a Black Standard and ride to the rescue of Quddús. Several hundred Bábís joined him and at Bárfurúsh the divines incited the townspeople to attack them. The Bábís beat off the attack and were given a promise of safe conduct away from the town. However, the divines broke their promise and tried to arrange for the murder of the entire company of Bábís. Mullá Ḥusayn and his companions took refuge in the lonely shrine of Shaykh Ṭabarsí and, though continually harassed, threw up a defensive mud wall around it.

When Bahá'u'lláh heard what had happened, He rode from Ṭihrán to the fort where He was reverently received by Mullá Ḥusayn and his companions. The loving encouragement Bahá'u'lláh gave to them lifted the spirits of the beleaguered Bábís. He advised them to seek the release of Quddús. It seemed highly unlikely that the authorities would, in the tense circumstances, agree to release Quddús but Bahá'u'lláh's advice was taken, His instructions followed and in due course Quddús joined his fellow-believers at Shaykh Ṭabarsí. Bahá'u'lláh had, in the meantime, left the fort, promising to return at a later date with more provisions. He travelled back to the capital through Núr.

Meanwhile the clamour of the divines of Bárfurúsh and the determination of the new Grand Vizier, Mírzá Taqí Khán, to suppress the Bábí movement, resulted in the despatch of troops to Shaykh Ṭabarsí. The Bábís defended themselves ably. More regiments were sent. Ill-equipped and untrained, Mullá Ḥusayn and his companions held out against overwhelming odds.

'In truth,' was the admission of one of the officers sent against them, 'I know not what had been shown to these people, or what they had seen, that they came forth to battle with such alacrity and joy . . . The imagination of man cannot conceive the vehemence of their courage and valour.'[2]

In December 1848 Bahá'u'lláh set out from Ṭihrán, intending to visit Shaykh Ṭabarsí a second time. He and His

Landscape in Mázindarán.

Shaykh Tabarsí.

companions were arrested while they were resting at a village only nine miles away from their goal and were taken to Ámul. The Governor of Ámul was with the troops besieging Shaykh Ṭabarsí. The Deputy Governor, uncertain how to deal with so eminent and distinguished a prisoner as Bahá'u'lláh, took Him and His companions into his own house.

When news spread through the town that a number of Bábís had been seized while on their way to join their companions at Shaykh Ṭabarsí, the whole town erupted in turmoil. The divines insisted that Bahá'u'lláh be brought to the mosque at once and incited the populace to gather there immediately and to bring knives, hatchets and axes with them. A mob of about four thousand crowded into the square of the mosque, the surrounding streets and the nearby rooftops. As many as could pushed their way inside the mosque. There, Bahá'u'lláh's calm and reasoned words silenced His critics but the angry divines were not satisfied. The Deputy Governor, in an attempt to hold in check the fierce and rising passions of the mob, ordered his attendants to prepare the rods used for the bastinado, a peculiarly savage form of punishment whereby people are beaten repeatedly with rods on the soles of their feet.

Bahá'u'lláh requested the Governor to punish Him alone and to spare His companions. His request was granted and in the presence of the mujtahids and siyyids of Ámul, Bahá'u'lláh received this humiliating and painful punishment. Even this did not appease the anger of the divines. They were still determined to kill Bahá'u'lláh. Bahá'u'lláh later related to Nabíl-i-A'ẓam that:

> The mullá and his followers . . . refused to believe Us, and rejected Our testimony as a perversion of the truth. They eventually placed Us in confinement, and forbade Our friends to meet Us. The acting governor of Ámul succeeded

> in effecting Our release from captivity. Through an opening in the wall that he ordered his men to make, he enabled Us to leave that room, and conducted Us to his house. No sooner were the inhabitants informed of this act than they arose against Us, besieged the governor's residence, pelted Us with stones, and hurled in Our face the foulest invectives.[3]

The Deputy Governor set his men, fully armed, in defensive positions and went out onto the roof, in full view of the mob. From there he shouted that Bahá'u'lláh was in his custody and that he would not release Him until he heard from the Governor.

The very next day a letter from the Governor arrived reprimanding his deputy for having arrested Bahá'u'lláh in the first place and threatening that if any harm came to Him he would not hesitate to burn down the whole town. When he arrived the next day, having abandoned the attack on Shaykh Ṭabarsí, he apologized profusely to Bahá'u'lláh and arranged for His safe escort, with His companions, back to Ṭihrán.

Throughout these tumultuous events, the Báb remained a prisoner, isolated from most of His followers. From His prison at Chihríq, the Báb directed all but three of His followers to hasten to the aid of Quddús, Mullá Ḥusayn and the other Bábís who were besieged at Shaykh Ṭabarsí. Ḥujjat, held in detention in Ṭihrán, fretted that he could not join his fellow-believers. Despite the official detention, Bahá'u'lláh was able to arrange for Ḥujjat to visit Him in Ṭihrán. Vaḥíd too, also unable to join his companions in the fort, visited Bahá'u'lláh's house in Ṭihrán from time to time. It was Bahá'u'lláh who strengthened their faith and deepened their understanding of the Báb's teachings, preparing them for the agonizing times that lay ahead of them both. Ṭáhirih, officially a prisoner in the house of the kalántar, also came to Bahá'u'lláh's house a number of times. When the siege of Shaykh Ṭabarsí became a massacre, it was Bahá'u'lláh who consoled and counselled the grieving Bábís.

The flower of the Báb's following, including nine of His first disciples, the Letters of the Living, perished at Shaykh Ṭabarsí. In early 1850 the esteemed Ḥájí Mírzá Siyyid 'Alí, the Báb's maternal uncle and the guardian of His childhood years, was brutally put to death in Ṭihrán along with six of the city's most distinguished citizens. At Nayríz and at Zanján the Bábís fought stubbornly against overwhelming odds to defend themselves and their families. At Nayríz, the Governor used treachery to break the siege, and in June Vaḥíd, renowned throughout the land for his learning and eloquence, was slaughtered with his companions. At Zanján, where the troubles had begun in May, the defenders held on.

Zanján, a small walled city, the capital of Khamsih province, is situated midway between Tabríz and Ṭihrán. It lies on a plain ringed around by mountains near to the river called the Zanján áb. There are villages here, scattered over the plain, and in winter and spring the powerful hill-tribes visit Zanján and the surrounding area. The old city was circular, built of sunburnt brick according to an ancient pattern: at the centre a fortress or citadel, and around it a maze of narrow cobbled streets and alleys, the whole encircled by a crenellated wall topped with high towers.

Zanján was, up to 1850, a relatively prosperous small city but in late May of 1850 the normal life of the area was totally disrupted. At the instigation of the local divines and on the order of its own Governor, the people of Zanján divided into two camps, those who followed the teachings of the Báb and those who opposed the new Faith. The Bábís, under the leadership of Ḥujjat, himself a former divine, took refuge in the citadel and an adjoining quarter of the town. The Governor ordered them to recant their faith or lose their lives.

The city was pitched into turmoil, families ripped apart, fields and businesses neglected. Ḥujjat and his companions, with the able and spirited support of their womenfolk, beat off the attacks the Governor and townspeople launched against them. Rumours circulated that there were at least ten thousand Bábís in the fort and that they were constantly receiving supplies but in reality Ḥujjat and his companions, numbering perhaps two thousand, together with women and children, were hard pressed and could obtain food only with great difficulty.

When news of the spirited and successful defence of the Bábís of Zanján reached Ṭihrán on 25 May, Mírzá Taqí Khán, the Grand Vizier, reacted with fury. Shaken and humiliated by the defeat which the imperial forces had suffered at Shaykh Ṭabarsí, he resolved to waste not one moment in stamping out what he saw as another dangerous Bábí uprising. He instantly despatched a battalion of infantry with four hundred horses and three guns to Zanján. At the same time he sent orders to two regiments already in Khamsih province to head for Zanján with all speed.

The Ṭihrán troops left only five hours after the first reports of trouble at Zanján reached the capital. The British Minister in Ṭihrán, Lt. Col Sheil, noted that this swift response was 'an instance unexampled in Persia of military celerity, which perhaps would not be surpassed in many countries of Europe'.[4] But once the troops reached Zanján they were unable to dislodge the Bábís from behind their hastily-erected barricades. A combined and prolonged attack by the townspeople, the volunteers recruited by the Governor from neighbouring villages and the regiments sent against them from Ṭihrán failed dismally.

The local populace, astonished at the zeal and courage of the Bábís, soon abandoned their efforts and left the job to the soldiers. Many of the officers made only half-hearted efforts for they too feared the determined defence they had encountered. A good number of the soldiers were members of the 'Alíyu'lláhí sect, a persecuted Islamic faction, and their sympathies lay more with the besieged than the besiegers. Some of the troops found highway robbery and molestation of the local inhabitants both less dangerous and more profitable than attempting to overcome the Bábís. Balked of military success, the thwarted and angry Governor constantly sent his town crier into the streets, calling upon the Bábís to desert Ḥujjat and promising to any deserter not only pardon and a safe passage but wealth and ennoblement.

In Ṭihrán, the Grand Vizier, growing ever more angry at the reports reaching him from Zanján, determined to uproot the very source of this dangerous heresy. He ordered the execution of the Báb, firmly believing that this would be the death blow of the whole troublesome movement. At noon on 9 July the Báb and His faithful companion Anís were executed and their shattered remains were thrown beyond the city walls. Sulaymán Khán, hurrying from Ṭihrán, was too late to attempt a rescue of the Báb but he did accomplish the rescue of the bodily remains from the edge of the moat where they had been thrown for wild dogs to consume.

As soon as Sulaymán Khán had the precious earthly remains of the Báb and Anís sealed into a casket and safely hidden near Tabríz, he sent word to Bahá'u'lláh in Ṭihrán. Bahá'u'lláh instructed His own brother Mírzá Músá to send a trustworthy messenger to bring the casket secretly from Tabríz to Ṭihrán. This perilous mission could not be carried out quickly. To avoid any suspicion, the casket was moved slowly, village by village, stage by stage, with the utmost secrecy and caution, through a hostile countryside.

CHAPTER 4

A SOMBRE EPISODE

THE news of the Báb's execution spread swiftly south from Tabríz to villages and towns and on across the mountains, plains and deserts to the distant scattered cities of Persia. The opponents of the new teachings rejoiced. The shocked, bewildered and grief-stricken Bábís mourned in silence and secrecy. When the bodies of the Báb and Anís disappeared from the edge of the moat, the divines eagerly spread the rumour abroad that they had been eaten by wild beasts.

The news of the Báb's execution and these accompanying rumours reached Zanján at a critical moment in the course of the long-drawn out and desperate siege. In July, with resources and supplies in the fort running low and with no end to the stalemate of the siege in sight, Ḥujjat decided to make a desperate appeal to the Sháh and urged his leading followers to do likewise.

'The subjects of your Imperial Majesty,' he wrote, 'regard you both as their temporal ruler and as the supreme custodian of their Faith. They appeal to you for justice . . . I and my principal companions hold ourselves in readiness to leave for Ṭihrán, that we may, in your presence as well as in that of our chief opponents, establish the soundness of our Cause.'[1]

But as Ḥujjat's messenger set out for Ṭihrán, he was seized and led before the Governor who ordered his immediate execution, destroyed the letters that he carried, substituted others loaded with abuse and insult and sent them, signed with Ḥujjat's name, to Ṭihrán. The Sháh, on reading these letters, angrily despatched two more regiments to Zanján together with the order that not one of Ḥujjat's supporters be allowed to survive.

It was while these messages were going to and fro that Siyyid Ḥasan, brother to the Báb's amanuensis, hastening away from the horrors of Tabríz, brought to Zanján the news of the Báb's execution. Faithful to the promise he had made to the Báb, he did not reveal his own faith. Unable, therefore, to throw in his lot with Ḥujjat and his companions, sick at heart at the wild delight which the news caused in the town, he hurried on towards Qazvín.

Armed with the news from Tabríz, the soldiers, whose skills had proved unequal to the daring and courage of the Bábís, and the frustrated and fearful townspeople, whose passions the divines had raised to fever pitch, loudly hurled their jubilant taunts at the beleaguered Bábís:

'For what reason', they cried out to the Bábís, 'will you henceforth be willing to sacrifice yourselves? He in whose path you long to lay down your lives, has himself fallen a victim to the bullets of a triumphant foe. His body is even now lost both to his enemies and to his friends. Why persist in your stubbornness when a word is sufficient to deliver you from your woes?'[2]

Their taunts had no effect whatever. Though stunned and grieved by the devastating news, Ḥujjat and his companions held firm to their faith. The siege of the Bábís at Zanján dragged on through the heat of summer. The commander-in-chief of the Sháh's forces, sent from Ṭihrán, now headed a force of seventeen regiments of cavalry and infantry and had at his disposal fourteen guns. But, despite their artillery and massive numerical superiority, the Sháh's armies were unable to subdue the Bábís and eject them from the frail protection which Zanján's small citadel and an adjacent quarter of the town afforded. The Grand Vizier, now frantic with impotent rage, sent a sharp warning to the commander-in-chief and the town's leaders.

'If your combined endeavours prove powerless to force their submission,' he threatened, 'I myself will proceed to Zanján, and will order a wholesale massacre of its inhabitants, irrespective of their position or belief. A town that can bring so much humiliation to the Sháh and distress to his people is utterly unworthy of the clemency of our sovereign.'[3]

These threats spurred the generals, the Governor and the divines to action. The townspeople were once again incited to join the soldiers in an assault on the fort and the adjoining section of the town into which the Bábís had barricaded themselves. In the fiercest fighting which had yet been experienced at Zanján many of Ḥujjat's most able companions died. Yet, against all reason and expectation, the Bábís still held their ground. The siege resumed and continued right through the autumn, the women valiantly supporting and assisting their menfolk, even cutting off their hair and using it as rope to bind the ramshackle cannons.

As the grip of the winter laid hold on the land, the commander-in-chief, faced with an increasing number of desertions amongst his demoralized troops, resorted to treachery. First he spread a rumour that the Sháh had decided to abandon the siege. Then he sent in to Ḥujjat an appeal for peace and a sealed copy of the Qur'án as a token of a solemn promise that the Bábís would not be harmed if they emerged from behind their barricades.

Ḥujjat responded to his plea by sending out a delegation composed of nine boys under ten years of age and a group of elderly men. At the commander-in-chief's headquarters the delegates were insulted and then attacked. Those who could fled back to the fort; the rest were savagely assaulted and thrown into prison.

Ḥujjat then urged all his companions to escape with their families under cover of darkness. A few followed this advice but the majority refused to leave him. The commander-in-chief, his treachery exposed, led sixteen regiments, each equipped with ten guns, in a furious month-long attack. Troop reinforcements poured into Zanján from all directions. Two more regiments, despatched by the Grand Vizier from Ṭihrán, arrived. The fort was subjected to an intense and continual bombardment with cannon. Three-quarters of the town already lay in ruins and the old brick walls of the fort could not long survive further battering. They began to crumble. Ḥujjat was hit by a bullet in the arm. His wound bled profusely. On hearing of this, his companions abandoned their posts at the barricades and hurried to him. The attackers redoubled their efforts and forced an entry into the fort, pillaging as they came and taking prisoner over a hundred women and children. The Bábís, their fighting strength now greatly reduced, crowded into the houses and buildings around Ḥujjat's residence, from which, despite a steady loss of life amongst the defenders, the exhausted and despairing troops were unable to dislodge them. Ḥujjat's wife and child were killed when a cannonball came through the wall of their shelter. Ḥujjat himself died nineteen days after receiving his wound. The Bábís demolished the room under which they buried him in a desperate attempt to conceal his resting-place.

News of Ḥujjat's death encouraged the troops to attempt yet one more assault. The remaining able-bodied Bábís, now less than two hundred, continued to fight in defence of their families until all of them were either slain or captured. The jubilant troops and townspeople, encouraged by the divines, slaughtered and pillaged. The wounded were herded into a roofless enclosure where they all soon died of exposure. The women and young girls were handed over to the troops; to the accompaniment of trumpets and drums, they were conducted to the army camp. Some of the captives, after being assured that their lives would be spared, were also given to the regiments who vied with each other in inventing and inflicting savage tortures upon the helpless Bábís. They were stripped naked, some were anointed with boiling oil, others with ice-cold water, some were blown from cannon, some smeared with treacle and left for dead in the snow, others were lashed mercilessly, then pierced with bayonets and lances. Not one amongst the Bábís recanted his faith or uttered a single word against his persecutors.

Ḥujjat's young son was tricked into revealing the whereabouts of his father's grave. The corpse was dug up, dragged through the streets to the sound of drums and trumpets and left in the main square, exposed to the insults and abuse of the townspeople. Forty-four of the most prominent of the male prisoners were dragged to prison in Ṭihrán.

The siege of Zanján had lasted, inexplicably, for seven months. In all, twenty thousand troops and nineteen pieces of artillery were used against the Bábís and about four and a half thousand troops died in their attempts to overcome the resistance of the two thousand Bábís and their families trapped in Zanján. The humiliation which the Bábís had inflicted on the imperial troops shook the government to its core. Accounts of the events at Zanján echoed through the capital and the court and rippled up and down the length and breadth of the country for months. On 2 March four of the prisoners from Zanján held in Ṭihrán were executed in public in the main square of Ṭihrán, the same square in which the Báb's uncle and six other Bábís had earlier perished.

CHAPTER 5

THE PROMISED ḤUSAYN

THE episode of Zanján cast a long, dark shadow over the land. In cities, towns and villages the infuriated and fearful divines provoked their followers to fresh harassment of the Bábís living amongst them. The Grand Vizier's rage was not yet appeased. In his zeal for revenge he tried every means in his power to find evidence that would enable him to label Bahá'u'lláh a Bábí and destroy Him also. He persisted in this search for months but all his efforts bore no fruit.

In late May or early June of 1851 he gave up. He summoned Bahá'u'lláh to appear before him at court and, in front of a large gathering, issued a clear warning. He was certain, he told Bahá'u'lláh, that without His support and guidance, the Bábís would never have held out for so long at Shaykh Ṭabarsí, at Nayríz and, most recently, at Zanján. It was regrettable, he continued, that Bahá'u'lláh had never devoted His superb and undoubted abilities to the service of the state, as His noble father had done. But, despite all that had passed, the Grand Vizier went on, he was now prepared to recommend to the Sháh that Bahá'u'lláh be appointed to the post of Amír-i-Díván, head of the Court. However, he advised Bahá'u'lláh, this was not an opportune moment to make such a recommendation as his Imperial Majesty was about to leave for Iṣfáhán. He recommended that, in the Sháh's absence, Bahá'u'lláh leave the capital.

These polite and courtly phrases amounted to an order. Bahá'u'lláh responded by refusing, in equally polite terms, the offer of employment and informed the Grand Vizier that He wished to make a pilgrimage to the holy cities of Najaf and Karbilá. Relieved and delighted, Mírzá Taqí Khán brought the interview to an end.

'Had the Amír-Niẓám', Bahá'u'lláh later stated, 'been aware of My true position, he would certainly have laid hold on Me. He exerted his utmost effort to discover the real situation, but was unsuccessful.'[1]

Just as Bahá'u'lláh was leaving Ṭihrán, the sealed casket containing the mortal remains of the Báb and Anís finally reached the capital. The hazardous journey from Tabríz had taken about ten months. It was solely due to Bahá'u'lláh's initiative, and in strict obedience to His instructions, that the precious remains reached Ṭihrán safely. As He left the city, Bahá'u'lláh gave instructions to Mírzá Músá and one other believer to hide the casket in the shrine of the Imám Zádih-Ḥasan near Ṭihrán. In the rising heat of summer, Bahá'u'lláh and two companions headed west towards 'Iráq.

Once over the seemingly endless plains and hills where the daytime sun flays travellers and the dust devils leap like demons over the dry land, they paused in the hilly coolness of Kirmánsháh. It was July and the month of Ramaḍán, the Muslim month of fasting.

Earlier, during the time that the Báb had been imprisoned at Chihríq, Bahá'u'lláh and one other Bábí had suggested to the Báb that Mírzá Yaḥyá, Bahá'u'lláh's young step-brother, be known as the appointed nominee of the Báb until such time as 'He Whom God shall make manifest' would appear. The Báb had agreed to this proposal. Now, from Kirmánsháh, Bahá'u'lláh sent Nabíl-i-A'ẓam to Ṭihrán with instructions to escort Mírzá Yaḥyá, who had reached there from Mázindarán, away from the dangers of the capital. Bahá'u'lláh asked Nabíl to remain with Mírzá Yaḥyá until such time as He could get back to Persia Himself. Nabíl, however, was unable to persuade Mírzá Yaḥyá to leave Ṭihrán.

When the Ramaḍán fast was over, Bahá'u'lláh and His

companions resumed their journey westward, down from the mountains and out across the flat, mud desert, travelling by night and resting by day away from the searing heat. On 28 August, after spending a few days in Baghdád, they reached Karbilá.

* * *

In the autumn of 1848, the Báb, imprisoned at Chihríq, on learning that Quddús and Mullá Ḥusayn were besieged at Shaykh Ṭabarsí, had urged all of His followers who were at Chihríq to go to their assistance. He had made only three exceptions. He had asked the two Bábí brothers of Yazd, Siyyid Ḥusayn and Siyyid Ḥasan, who had been with Him since His arrival in Ádharbáyján, to remain with Him and He had asked Shaykh Ḥasan-i-Zunúzí to travel to Karbilá and to remain there.

Shaykh Ḥasan had attained the presence of the Báb in Karbilá, before the Báb declared His mission. 'That Youth', he later recounted, 'had set my heart aflame . . . My soul was wedded to His till the day when the call of a Youth from Shíráz . . . reached my ears.'[2]

When the Báb returned to Shíráz from His pilgrimage to Mecca, Shaykh Ḥasan attained His presence and acknowledged his belief in Him. He preceded the Báb to Iṣfáhán and was one of the very few believers allowed into His presence there. So great was Shaykh Ḥasan's love for the Báb that he could not remain far from Him. He visited the Báb at Kulayn and followed Him northwards, all the way to Tabríz and beyond. He was admitted to the Báb's presence during His detention in Tabríz, was the first Bábí to reach Máh-Kú and the first pilgrim to gain admittance to the fortress. When the Báb was transferred to Chihríq, he followed and when the Báb was summoned to the clerical convocation in Tabríz, Shaykh Ḥasan went to that city.

Well aware of Shaykh Ḥasan's devotion and outstanding constancy, the Báb gave him a special mission:

'You should proceed', He said, 'to Karbilá and should abide in that holy city, inasmuch as you are destined to behold, with your own eyes, the beauteous countenace of the promised Ḥusayn. As you gaze upon that radiant face, do also remember Me. Convey to Him the expression of My loving devotion . . . I have entrusted you with a great mission. Beware lest your heart grow faint, lest you forget the glory with which I have invested you.'[3]

Shaykh Ḥasan sorrowfully bade farewell to the Báb but faithfully obeyed His instructions. He travelled to Karbilá where he had lived only a few years previously as a student of Shaykh Aḥmad and Siyyid Káẓim. Fearful that a prolonged visit to the city might arouse the suspicions of the divines and his former fellow-students, those followers of Shaykh Aḥmad and Siyyid Káẓim who had not recognized the Báb, he married and settled in the city, earning his living as a scribe. Worn and frail now, Shaykh Ḥasan lived patiently in near penury, telling no one why he was there, enduring the scorn and contempt of the Shaykhís, his former companions. He learnt, with inexpressible grief, of the brutal execution of his beloved master in Tabríz and mourned Him in secrecy.

Shaykh Ḥasan had lived quietly in Karbilá for two years when, in early October of 1851, as he later recounted to Nabíl-i-A'ẓam,

> . . . while I was passing by the gate of the inner courtyard of the shrine of the Imám Ḥusayn, my eyes, for the first time, fell upon Bahá'u'lláh. What shall I recount regarding the countenance which I beheld! The beauty of that face, those exquisite features which no pen or brush dare describe, His penetrating glance, His kindly face, the majesty of His bearing, the sweetness of His smile, the luxuriance of His jet-black flowing locks, left an indelible impression upon my

soul. I was then an old man, bowed with age. How lovingly He advanced towards me! He took me by the hand and, in a tone which at once betrayed power and beauty, addressed me in these words: 'This very day I have purposed to make you known as a Bábí throughout Karbilá.' Still holding my hand in His, He continued to converse with me. He walked with me all along the market-street, and in the end He said: 'Praise be to God that you have remained in Karbilá, and have beheld with your own eyes the countenance of the promised Ḥusayn.'[4]

On hearing these words, Shaykh Ḥasan instantly recalled the promise given to him by the Báb. Moved to the very depths of his being and filled with an overwhelming joy, he yearned to cry out, there and then, to all the city, that the Báb's promise was indeed fulfilled.

'Not yet,' Bahá'u'lláh cautioned him lovingly, 'the appointed Hour is approaching. It has not yet struck. Rest assured and be patient.'[5]

Just five weeks after Bahá'u'lláh met with Shaykh Ḥasan in Karbilá, the Grand Vizier, Mírzá Taqí Khán, was toppled from power. The young, unstable and inexperienced Náṣiri'd-Dín Sháh owed his very throne to the efforts of Mírzá Taqí Khán and had married one of his own sisters to his powerful chief minister. However, the Sháh's mother swiftly grew jealous of Mírzá Taqí Khán's influence over her son. Mírzá Áqá Khán, a prominent figure at court, was also bitterly jealous of the Grand Vizier and together he and the Sháh's mother sowed seeds of doubt and suspicion in the Sháh's mind, arousing his jealousy.

Thus on 13 November 1851 Náṣiri'd-Dín Sháh summarily dismissed Mírzá Taqí Khán from office and banished him to Káshán. It is related that a petition submitted by the Russian minister on behalf of the deposed minister further angered the Sháh and provoked him into sending a courtier to Káshán with orders to murder secretly his former chief minister. The young princess, Mírzá Taqí Khán's wife, against the entreaties of her mother, insisted on accompanying her disgraced husband to Káshán. There she prepared all his food and he left the house only in her company. But after two months, by careful scheming, the Sháh's emissary managed to entice Mírzá Taqí Khán to visit the public bath alone. He then crept into the bath-house and told Mírzá Taqí Khán of his orders. Mírzá Taqí Khán chose the manner of his own death and met his end bravely as his veins were cut open.

Mírzá Áqá Khán-i-Núrí, just as he had hoped, promptly succeeded to the position of Grand Vizier. The new chief minister came from the same area of Mázindarán as did Bahá'u'lláh and was distantly related to Him. During the time that Ḥáji Mírzá Áqásí had been Grand Vizier, Mírzá Áqá Khán had fallen out of favour at court, had been fined, bastinadoed and banished from the court to Káshán. Bahá'u'lláh had paid a considerable part of the fine for him, had helped him to obtain an annual annuity and had arranged for his children to travel to Káshán.

While the court and the country adjusted itself to the regime of a new chief minister, Bahá'u'lláh remained quietly in Karbilá. He had found the Bábís of that city in a sad condition, leaderless, confused and dispirited. His presence revived their spirits and restored their hopes: His fearless advocacy of the Cause of the Báb gave them new courage. Patiently and lovingly He deepened their understanding of the Báb's message, refocused their energies and helped them to hold steadfastly to the assurances of the Báb that 'He Whom God shall make manifest' would, in God's good time, make His appearance.

Mírzá Áqá Khán, the new Grand Vizier, decided, at the outset of his ministry, to seek a reconciliation between the government and Bahá'u'lláh. In the spring of 1852 he sent a warm and friendly letter to Bahá'u'lláh requesting His return to Ṭihrán and expressing his eagerness to meet Him again. But even before this letter arrived in 'Iráq Bahá'u'lláh had already decided to return.

The clouds of hatred, bigotry and fanaticism hung low over His homeland, drawing up fresh strength and violence for a new and terrible assault. Bahá'u'lláh rode unafraid into the eye of the storm.

CHAPTER 6
CALAMITY

BAHÁ'U'LLÁH arrived back in Ṭihrán in late April or early May of 1852. The Grand Vizier sent his own brother, Ja'far-Qulí-Khán, to welcome Him and to offer Him hospitality at his country home in Lavásán, for the summer heat in the city was excessive. Bahá'u'lláh accepted the offer to stay at Ja'far-Qulí-Khán's home as a guest of the chief minister. So many people, notables, officials and dignitaries of the capital came to visit Him there that He was unable to return to His own home for several weeks. It was while He was in Lavásán, at some point during these weeks, that Bahá'u'lláh learnt of an imminent danger threatening the entire Bábí community.

A certain Bábí named Mullá Shaykh-'Alí, known as 'Aẓím, from Khurásán, was living in Ṭihrán. 'Aẓím had gathered around him a cluster of aggrieved Bábís who blamed the Sháh himself for all the calamities that had fallen upon their community. Amongst the group were three hot-headed and impetuous youths: Ṣádiq, a confectioner of Tabríz; Fatḥu'lláh, an engraver from Qum; and Ḥájí Qásim of Nayríz. The minds of all three had been unhinged by the cruel execution of the Báb. 'Aẓím and his companions met in various houses in Ṭihrán, including that of Ḥájí Sulaymán Khán, the brilliant young courtier who had arranged for the rescue of the bodily remains of the Báb and Anís from Tabríz. Together they hatched a plot to assassinate the Sháh.

'Aẓím had sought for a long time to speak with Bahá'u'lláh and obtain His support for this scheme. During the weeks that Bahá'u'lláh was a guest of the Grand Vizier, while He was making a short journey to Shimrán, 'Aẓim managed to speak with Him. As soon as 'Aẓim revealed what was intended, Bahá'u'lláh warned him in no uncertain terms of the extreme danger and stupidity of such a scheme. He roundly condemned the conspirators and warned that any such insane treachery would bring unimaginable catastrophe to the entire Bábí community. He would, He said, have nothing whatsoever to do with so despicable a plan and He warned 'Aẓím to abandon any such scheme immediately. 'Aẓím ignored His advice.

On the morning of 15 August the Sháh rode out from his summer palace at Níyávarán, intending to go hunting. Some distance ahead of him, sufficiently far in front so that the dust they raised would not inconvenience him, rode equerries carrying long lances, grooms leading horses with embroidered saddle cloths and a group of nomad riders, rifles slung over their shoulders, swords hanging from their saddles. The king proceeded slowly on his own. A respectful distance behind him, ready to halt whenever he did, followed his customary retinue of lords, chiefs and officers.

The Sháh had only just left the palace grounds when he noticed three men waiting to address him, one on the right hand side of the narrow roadway, two on the left. This was not unusual, for it was a custom that any subject of the Sháh might approach his presence respectfully and submit a petition directly to him. The Sháh rode forward, unsuspecting of any danger. He saw the young men bow low as he approached and heard them, in unison, make the customary appeal, 'We are your sacrifice! We make a request!'

But then, instead of waiting submissively for a royal response, the three youths rushed forward, repeating their cry, 'We make a request!' As his startled horse plunged beneath him, the Sháh cried out, 'Rascals, what do you want?' Ṣádiq fired a round of buckshot at the Sháh, wounding him slightly. The wounds were only skin deep. Then he seized the king's right leg and tried to pull him off his horse. He could not succeed for Fatḥu'lláh and Ḥájí Qásim were pulling at the king's left leg. As his horse plunged and reared, the king hit out with his fists at the heads of his assailants.

The royal retinue, momentarily stunned into inaction by so appalling and unexpected a sight, now rushed forward. The S͟háh's ministers, headed by the Grand Vizier, beat off the attackers. Ṣádiq was killed instantly by the grand equerry and a nomad outrider who had raced back to the side of the S͟háh. Several lords threw Fatḥu'lláh and Ḥájí Qásim to the ground and bound them securely. The court physician then led the S͟háh into a nearby walled garden in order to attend to his wounds. These were slight, for the half-crazed youths had not armed themselves with shot that would kill a man. However, the tumult that arose in and around Níyávarán in the next hour was extreme. As the S͟háh's ministers all crowded into the garden to attend on the royal personage, a rumour began outside the garden walls that the S͟háh had been killed. Bugles, drums, tambourines and fifes summoned the royal troops. Orders were shouted but no one knew what was really happening. The royal camp began to break up and crowds of people started to run towards Ṭihrán.

When the crowds and the rumours reached the city, the shopkeepers closed their shops. Almost everyone left the streets but the bakeries were besieged all night long as people, anticipating troubled days ahead, tried to buy food. At dawn of the next day, as the agitation grew, the Governor set troops to patrol the deserted streets, barred the gates of both the city and the citadel, charged his batteries, put the regiment stationed there onto a war footing and pointed his loaded guns at the as yet unknown enemy.

The next morning, as salutes of one hundred and ten guns

were fired, the clergy and the civil officers of state and the troops camped near Ṭihrán were all summoned to view the <u>Sh</u>áh. The <u>Sh</u>áh then proceeded in great pomp to the mosque in Ṭihrán and there gave thanks for his miraculous escape. Next, his ministers and the Russian, English and Ottoman ambassadors, in full court dress, attended him to offer their congratulations. Public rejoicing was organized and by night the city was illuminated. However, Lt. Col Sheil relates that the <u>Sh</u>áh and his entire Court, as well as the Russian Mission, left their summer residences on the mountain slopes and sought safety within the city a month before the usual season, in spite of the insalubrity of the climate. Lady Sheil wrote more graphically: 'The panic at Shemeroon became general; no one thought himself safe unless within the walls of Tehran. Every bush was a Bábee, or concealed one. Shah, ministers, meerzas, soldiers, priests, merchants, all went pell-mell into Tehran . . .'[1]

Apparently, there was more to be feared from the Bábís than from the cholera which raged in the cities of Persia that year and an outbreak of which, in normal times, could empty a city in hours.

The <u>Sh</u>áh was mortified that he had been forced to struggle alone for some minutes without any help from his guards and retinue. Incensed by the attack, he was convinced of a deep-seated and dangerous conspiracy and was determined to seek out and punish all the plotters. On 17 August, just two days after the attack, Lt. Col Sheil and Prince Dolgorouki, the Russian ambassador, addressed a joint letter to the <u>Sh</u>áh appealing to him not to allow those found guilty of conspiracy against him to be tortured before their executions:

The Undersigned have heard with the deepest pain that an intention exists of inflicting torture, previously to execution on the wretches who were guilty of a treasonable and horrible

> attempt on the person of His Majesty with the design of extorting a confession of their confederates. Infamous as has been their crime, the Undersigned trust that such outrage on common sense will not be allowed to happen. If in their agonies these criminals should utter the names of certain individuals, can it be believed that they will betray their friends and companions. Is it not certain that they will accuse persons wholly innocent, and that no end will be gained excepting to fill the mind of his Majesty the Shah with suspicion against blameless persons.[2]

Their appeal fell on deaf ears. The opportunity to stamp out, once and for all, the Bábí heresy, was at hand. The public horror, disgust and resentment at the incident could now be turned against the entire Bábí community, men, women and children. Fatḥu'lláh and Ḥájí Qásim were subjected to intense questioning. When they would not give the names of their fellow-conspirators, they were tortured with red-hot pincers and limb-rending screws. Fatḥu'lláh uttered not a single word and was taken to be deaf and dumb. He died as molten lead was poured down his throat. Ṣádiq's body was tied to the tail of a mule and dragged to Ṭihrán where it was hewn into two halves and hung over the city gate. The civil authorities then invited the citizens of Ṭihrán to view the mutilated corpse from the ramparts. Ḥájí Qásim was later executed in Shimrán.

The Governor of Ṭihrán picketed the gates of the capital and ordered his guards to scrutinize all who left. The Grand Vizier summoned to his presence the mayor of Ṭihrán and other minor officials. He ordered them to search out and arrest anyone, man or woman, suspected of being a Bábí. 'Abbás, the servant of 'Aẓím, in whose house the conspirators had met, was coerced into denouncing any individual thought likely to offer a bribe in order to secure his freedom.

Bahá'u'lláh was still a guest of the Grand Vizier Mírzá Áqá Khán when the news of the assassination attempt reached

Him and was still staying at the country residence owned by Ja'far-Qulí-Khán in the village of Afchih, in Lavásán. Ja'far-Qulí-Khán was at Shimrán when the attack occurred. When he heard the news he immediately sent a trusted messenger to Bahá'u'lláh with a letter urging Him to go into hiding at once and to remain hidden until things calmed down. His own servant, he promised, would accompany his guest to a place of safety.

'The Sháh's mother', he wrote, 'is inflamed with anger. She is denouncing you openly before the court and people as the "would-be murderer" of her son. She is also trying to involve Mírzá Áqá Khán in this affair, and accuses him of being your accomplice.'[3]

The Grand Vizier also wrote to Bahá'u'lláh warning of the Sháh's mother's anger and desire for revenge.

Bahá'u'lláh received the letters but courteously rejected the advice. The next morning He rode from Lavásán to the army camp at Níyávarán. A short distance from the camp, in the village of Zargandih, He passed the Russian Legation and was met by His brother-in-law, Mírzá Majíd, who worked as secretary to the Russian minister. Mírzá Majíd invited Bahá'u'lláh to enter his house, which adjoined the Legation.

Bahá'u'lláh's presence, so near to the army headquarters, was a cause of astonishment to all and word of His arrival quickly reached the Sháh.

The Sháh at once sent an officer to the Russian Legation to demand that Bahá'u'lláh be delivered into his hands. The Russian minister refused and asked that Bahá'u'lláh be allowed to proceed to the home of Mírzá Áqá Khán, whose guest He still was. This request was granted. The Russian minister then addressed a formal communication to the Grand Vizier, expressing his desire that every possible care be taken to secure the safety and protection of Bahá'u'lláh. His government, the minister warned, would hold Mírzá

Áqá Khán personally responsible if any harm should befall his guest.

Mírzá Áqá Khán received Bahá'u'lláh into his own house with the most fulsome assurances. However, when the Sháh, urged on by the clamour of the clergy and the prompting of his own mother, demanded that Bahá'u'lláh be arrested, Mírzá Áqá Khán gave in and meekly handed over his guest to the Sháh's officers. At Níyávarán Bahá'u'lláh was bastinadoed and then hustled, on foot and in chains, a distance of about fifteen kilometres, to Ṭihrán. His turban, the token of His noble lineage, was snatched from Him and during the journey His outer garments were stripped from Him. As He was brought into Ṭihrán and led towards the dungeon, He was mocked, abused and pelted with stones. Among the crowd was an old woman, frail and decrepit but frenzied with rage. She was trying to hurl a stone but could not keep pace with the soldiers. Bahá'u'lláh, hearing her plead with the guard to slow down, Himself appealed to the soldiers.

'Suffer not this woman', He asked, 'to be disappointed. Deny her not what she regards as a meritorious act in the sight of God.'[4]

Ásíyih Khánum and her children were at their home in Ṭihrán when the news of Bahá'u'lláh's arrest reached them. A servant of the household, rushing in urgent distress from the street, broke the news.

'The master, the master, he is arrested – I have seen him! He has walked many miles! Oh, they have beaten him! They say he has suffered the torture of the bastinado! His feet are bleeding! He has no shoes on! His turban has gone! His clothes are torn! There are chains upon his neck!'[5]

Everyone in that great household – relatives, friends and servants alike – scattered to safety. Only Mírzá Músá, Bahá'u'lláh's brother, and two servants, both of African origin, a man and a woman, remained with Ásíyih Khánum.

Ásíyih Khánum only had time to snatch up a few valuable possessions and hurry the children before her out of the house and into the relative obscurity of the streets before a mob bent on pillage and destruction burst in. Mírzá Músá helped Ásíyih Khánum to find a hiding place in a little house not far from the prison and then went into hiding himself.

Bahá'u'lláh was led past crowds of jeering onlookers to the Síyáh-Chál, the Black Pit, a notorious prison in the southern part of the city. This dreadful place, originally an outlet for the waste waters of a public bath, damp, putrid, foul-smelling, verminous and cold as a tomb even in the heat of summer, housed the capital's most notorious and dangerous criminals.

CHAPTER 7

A DARK AND DREADFUL HOUR

BAHÁ'U'LLÁH has Himself described His arrival at the Síyáh-Chál:

> Upon Our arrival We were first conducted along a pitch-black corridor, from whence We descended three steep flights of stairs to the place of confinement assigned to Us. The dungeon was wrapped in thick darkness, and Our fellow-prisoners numbered nearly a hundred and fifty souls: thieves, assassins and highwaymen. Though crowded, it had no other outlet than the passage by which We entered. No pen can depict that place, nor any tongue describe its loathsome smell. Most of these men had neither clothes nor bedding to lie on.[1]

Bahá'u'lláh was chained to five other Bábís in a small cell crowded with prisoners. The chains were secured in a way that prevented the prisoners from either sitting up straight, standing or lying down. Every time that one person attempted to move, the chains would cut into his own flesh and that of his fellow-sufferers. Around Bahá'u'lláh's neck were placed alternately the two most dreaded prison chains of the country. Under their heavy weight, His whole frame was bent. Later, He wrote of this prolonged torture:

> Shouldst thou at some time happen to visit the dungeon of His Majesty the Sháh, ask the director and chief jailer to show thee those two chains, one of which is known as Qará-Guhar, and the other as Salásil. I swear by the Day-Star of Justice that for four months this Wronged One was tormented and chained by one or the other of them.[2]

For three days and nights the Bábí prisoners were given no food or drink. Sleep was impossible for them on a floor that was ankle-deep in filth. Worst of all were the horror and shame they felt at the terrible blot inflicted on the name of their beloved Faith, the knowledge of the grave dangers now facing the entire community and the anxiety they experienced for their families and fellow-believers in the city above them. Their fears were well founded for within a week the executions began.

Ṭáhirih, the only woman amongst the Báb's chosen disciples, a poetess, renowned in Persia and neighbouring 'Iráq for her purity of character, her brilliant intellect and her fearless devotion to the Cause of the Báb, was strangled and her body thrown into a disused well where stones were heaped upon it. She went to her death as a bride to her wedding, in her finest white apparel, perfumed and exquisitely groomed, radiantly calm and confident. 'You can kill me as soon as you like' she declared to her executioners, 'but you cannot stop the emancipation of women.'[3]

A certain Dr Jakob Polak, resident in Ṭihrán in 1852, claimed to have been present at Ṭáhirih's execution: 'I was an eyewitness', he later wrote, 'of the execution of Qurratu'l-'Ayn, the Minister for War and his adjutant performed it. That beautiful lady suffered her slow death with superhuman fortitude.'[4]

Ḥájí Sulaymán Khán, in whose house the conspirators had occasionally assembled, whose prestige in court circles had preserved him from punishment as a Bábí on a previous occasion, was now arrested. The Sháh and his chief minister attempted to induce him to recant his faith in the Báb but the young courtier refused. The Sháh then ordered that he be put to death but allowed him to choose the manner of his execution. Sulaymán Khán asked that nine holes be cut into his flesh and a lighted candle be inserted into each. Preceded by minstrels and drummers, straight as an arrow, his eyes glowing with a zealous love, unmoved by the howling of the mob that surged about him or the blood that streamed down his body, he led the way to his own execution. Every few steps he stopped to utter praises of the Báb and to exult in his own martyrdom. Whenever a candle fell from his body, he would pick it up, relight it from the others and replace it.

'Why dost thou not dance', mocked the executioner, 'since thou findest death so pleasant?'

'Dance?' cried Ḥájí Sulaymán Khán. 'In one hand the wine-cup, in one hand the tresses of the Friend. Such a dance in the midst of the market-place is my desire!'

As the flames of the candles burnt deep into his sizzling flesh, he cried out: 'You have long lost your sting, O flames, and have been robbed of your power to pain me. Make haste, for from your very tongues of fire I can hear the voice that calls me to my Beloved.'

In a blaze of light he strode to his death. At the foot of the gallows, he addressed a final appeal to the onlookers. He then prostrated himself in prayer and afterwards called to the executioner: 'My work is now finished, come and do yours.'

His body, while still alive, was sawn into two halves and suspended, as he had requested, on either side of a gate into the city. It was on the same day, and in the same manner, that Ḥájí Qásim, the only one of the three attackers of the Sháh still alive, met his death in Shimrán. On 22 August Lt. Col Sheil reported that about ten persons had been publicly executed, some in circumstances of great cruelty. When the Bábí victims had been put to death, their bodies were handed over to the mob.

The prison jailers carried news of these events into the Síyáh-Chál. The executioners, hardened by the requirements of their daily work but deeply affected by the stoic fortitude of the Bábís, began to befriend their Bábí prisoners. One of them, moved by the pitiable plight of Bahá'u'lláh, offered Him tea, but Bahá'u'lláh refused it.

Bahá'u'lláh later recounted to Nabíl-i-A'ẓam the agony and exultation of those days:

> All those who were struck down by the storm that raged during that memorable year in Ṭihrán were Our fellow-prisoners in the Síyáh-Chál, where We were confined. We were all huddled together in one cell, our feet in stocks, and around our necks fastened the most galling of chains. The air we breathed was laden with the foulest impurities, while the floor on which we sat was covered with filth and infested with vermin. No ray of light was allowed to penetrate that pestilential dungeon or to warm its icy-coldness. We were placed in two rows, each facing the other. We had taught them to repeat certain verses which, every night, they chanted with extreme fervour. 'God is sufficient unto me; He verily is the All-sufficing!' one row would intone, while the other would reply: 'In Him let the trusting trust.' The chorus of these gladsome voices would continue to peal out until the early hours of the morning. Their reverberation would fill the dungeon, and, piercing its massive walls, would reach the ears of Náṣiri'd-Dín Sháh, whose palace was not far distant from the place where we were imprisoned. 'What means this sound?' he was reported to have exclaimed. 'It is the anthem the Bábís are intoning in their prison,' they replied. The Sháh made no further remarks, nor did he attempt to restrain the enthusiasm his prisoners, despite the horrors of their confinement, continued to display.[5]

Mírzá Áqá Khán, the Grand Vizier, had intended to inaugurate his ministry by bringing about a reconciliation between his government and the followers of the Báb but the attack on the Sháh shattered any such plans. The Grand Vizier, knowing full well that persecution would only fan the flames of the new Faith, at first counselled leniency, but the Sháh was too angry to listen to such advice. Driven by the rage of the Sháh himself, the furious and insatiable desire for vengeance of the Sháh's mother and the implacable hostility of the clergy towards the Bábís, the Grand Vizier was forced to act against his better judgement.

He was, however, nervous of the long-term repercussions of the savage action he was about to take. He hit upon a novel plan whereby the responsibility for putting the Bábís to death would be shouldered by the entire regime. Lt. Col Sheil reported to the British government on 27 August:

> This Court has within the last few days presented the extraordinary and disgraceful spectacle of all the Chief Officers of State being converted into Executioners. Each department of the government has had a victim among the conspirators, or supposed conspirators, against the King's life . . .
>
> My remonstrances with the Sedr Azim [chief minister] against the disgrace which he was heaping on the reputation of the Persian Government and nation were taken in very ill part. He asked me if I wanted to place the responsibility of so many executions on him alone and bring down Bábee vengeance on himself and his family.[6]

The entire machinery of government was directed to the task of tracking down and arresting any known or suspected Bábís, regardless of whether or not they were implicated in the conspiracy. The Grand Vizier then divided the work of execution amongst the royal princes, nobles, principal ministers, generals and officers of the court, the clergy and merchants, the artillery and infantry. Two Bábís were to die each day, one in Ṭihrán and one in Shimrán, both in the same manner. The Sháh himself was allocated a victim but he chose to delegate the actual duty of killing a Bábí to the steward of his household. Even the Sháh's French physician, Dr Cloquet, was invited to join in the killing but he managed to excuse himself, as Lady Sheil recounts, by explaining that he killed too many men professionally to allow him to increase their number by voluntary homicide on his part. The priesthood and the students of the college of Arts and Sciences founded by the late Mírzá Taqí Khán were also called upon to participate. The highest ecclesiastical dignitary in the city, the Imám-Jum'ih, personally executed one victim. The only person exempted from the grisly work was the Grand Vizier himself.

All those arrested were first thrown into the city dungeons and were then distributed among these various groups of people, whose messengers would visit the dungeons daily to claim their victims. Eighty-one known and suspected Bábís were imprisoned in the Síyáh-Chál with Bahá'u'lláh. They represented all classes of the city's society. Thirty-eight of them were leading members of the community. Bahá'u'lláh later related to Nabíl,

> Every day Our gaolers, entering Our cell, would call the name of one of Our companions, bidding him arise and follow them to the foot of the gallows. With what eagerness would the owner of that name respond to that solemn call! Relieved of his chains, he would spring to his feet and, in a state of uncontrollable delight, would approach and embrace Us. We would seek to comfort him with the assurance of an everlasting life in the world beyond, and, filling his heart with hope and joy, would send him forth to win the crown of glory. He would embrace, in turn, the rest of his fellow-prisoners, and then proceed to die as dauntlessly as he had lived. Soon after the martyrdom of each of these companions, We would be informed by the executioner, who had grown to be friendly to Us, of the circumstances of the death of his victim, and of the joy with which he had endured his sufferings to the very end.[7]

Siyyid Ḥusayn-i-Yazdí, the Báb's amanuensis and trusted companion, a man of merit and renown, refused the offers of safety made to him by the city's leading officials and was hacked to pieces by the highest officers in the Sháh's army. Ḥájí Mírzá Jání, the respected merchant of Káshán, in whose house the Báb had celebrated Naw-Rúz, was battered to death by the leading merchants and traders of the capital. Áqá Muḥammad Taqí, a native of S̲h̲íráz, was handed over to the royal Master of Horse and his men. They first skinned his feet, then soaked them in boiling oil, then shod him with iron shoes and made him run to the scaffold. There he was beaten to death with maces and the great iron nails to which the horses were fastened in their stables. Muḥammad 'Alí of Najafábád was handed over to the artillery who first tore out one of his eyes, then bound him over the muzzle of a cannon and blew him to pieces. The young students of the College of Arts and Sciences cut down a learned man of Damávand, Mírzá Nabí, with swords and spears. The names of these and others executed were recorded in the official gazette of Ṭihrán.

Once the hunt for Bábís was well launched, the slaughter intensified. Ásíyih K̲h̲ánum, hiding with her young children in a darkened house, heard the howling mobs surge through the surrounding streets in pursuit of their quarry. She could only venture out on the streets late at night, for women and children were not spared in the hunt. Only one relative by marriage, the wife of a Russian subject and a friend of the Russian minister, dared to visit her. This woman's husband attended the courts each day to hear who was next condemned to death and passed on this news through his wife. With his help, Ásíyih K̲h̲ánum was able to get food for Bahá'u'lláh into the Síyáh-C̲h̲ál. In order to do this, she sold the few valuable possessions that she had snatched up when hurrying from her home.

The new Faith had spread through all ranks and classes in the city from the highest to the lowest. Those from simple and humble backgrounds were speedily handed over to the torturers and executioners who vied with each other in devising novel and ever more cruel methods of despatching their victims out of this world. Eyes were gouged out, ears amputated and forced down the throats of their one-time owners, teeth were ripped out and bare skulls battered with hammers. Bodies were slowly strangled, hacked into pieces, blown from cannons, slashed, bayoneted and stoned. When life was finally extinguished, some scorched and perforated corpses were hung head downward in trees so that any who willed might use them as targets for practising their marksmanship. Others were hacked in two and hung at the city gates, still others were tossed out into the plain as food for dogs and jackals.

'I saw', an Austrian officer wrote in a letter dated 29 August, 'corpses torn by nearly 150 bullets . . . At present I never leave my house, in order not to meet with fresh scenes of horror . . .'[8]

Sometimes the corpses were handed over to the mob who fell upon them like ravening beasts, tore them limb from limb or mutilated them beyond any recognition of their original form. The executioners, hardened to their own grisly work, were yet astonished at the ferocity of the people.

The *Journal de Constantinople*, as quoted by the London *Morning Post*, stated that the executions of 'about 400 Babis, who are said to have been accomplices of the attempt against the Shah of Persia took place in a very cruel manner. They were subjected to the greatest tortures."[9]

But the dauntless courage of the Bábís began to have its effect. Once the initial horror and indignation at the assassination attempt were overcome, the blood-letting began to backfire. As Lady Sheil reported, 'Indignation at the attempt on the Shah's life was lost in sympathy for the fate of so many sufferers.'[10]

On one occasion a crowd watched in awed silence as men, women and children, with lighted wicks soaked in oil stuck in gaping, streaming wounds were dragged by cords and driven by whips to their death. Their chanting voices rose piercingly through that silence as they sang, 'Verily from God we come, and unto Him we return!'[11] Some of the children died as they walked. The executioners threw their bodies under the feet of their parents, brothers and sisters. When the survivors of the march arrived at the place of execution, life was again offered to them if they would only recant. Children were killed in front of their parents. At nightfall the mangled remains of the bodies were tossed in heaps for the dogs of the city to consume.

The persecution was not confined to Ṭihrán. In every locality the divines encouraged their followers to take action against the Bábís. At Mílán, near Tabríz, a number of Bábís were killed and others dragged to a prison in the city. On 7 September, Stevens, the British agent, reported from Tabríz that 'the recent religious persecutions and executions at Tehran have created very general disgust here.'[12]

The Sh͟áh's mother was determined that Bahá'u'lláh too should die and openly denounced Him as the would-be murderer of her son.

'Deliver him to the executioner!' she raged. 'What greater humiliation than this, that I, who am the mother of the Sh͟áh, should be powerless to inflict upon that criminal the punishment so dastardly an act deserves!'[13]

'Abbás, the servant of the conspirator 'Aẓím, had been forced, under the threat of inhuman torture, to walk the streets of the city and point out all those whom he recognized as Bábís. Now he was brought into the Síyáh-C͟hál, day after day, face-to-face with Bahá'u'lláh, and was asked to identify Him as one of those who had met in his master's house. Despite the offer of a substantial reward from the Sh͟áh's mother, every time 'Abbás was brought into the presence of Bahá'u'lláh he adamantly maintained that he had never seen Him in the company of the other Bábís. Then the Sh͟áh's mother and her allies tried to poison Bahá'u'lláh by intercepting the food that His family sent to Him in the prison and mixing poison into it. The poison made Him very ill and damaged His health for years to come but did not kill Him. Thwarted in their desire to promptly execute Bahá'u'lláh, His enemies turned their attention to His properties in Tákur.

Mírzá Yaḥyá, young and impressionable, had been certain that the conspirators' plan to assassinate the Sháh would succeed. Sometime in the summer of 1852, before 15 August, he moved from Ṭihrán to Tákur in order to consolidate his own leadership there and to stir up a rising timed to coincide with the assassination attempt. He managed to persuade a few of the Bábís to put on fighting gear and take up arms. Rumours that the Bábís of Tákur were planning an uprising began to spread. When news of the failure of the assassination attempt reached Núr, Mírzá Yaḥyá, terrified for his own life, fled in disguise towards Rasht. Bahá'u'lláh's uncle, hostile to the new Faith, sent to Ṭihrán exaggerated accounts of a Bábí uprising and the Grand Vizier promptly sent his own nephew and a troop of soldiers to Tákur to deal with the situation. He and his troops terrorized the neighbourhood, devastated a large area of the countryside, sacked and pillaged Bahá'u'lláh's mansion and levelled every house in the village. Twenty of the leading Bábís were taken to the Síyáh-Chál where six of them perished in the presence of Bahá'u'lláh. The Grand Vizier confiscated, without authority or recompense, a number of Bahá'u'lláh's properties and transferred them to his own name.

In Ṭihrán, relatives, friends and admirers of Bahá'u'lláh sought by every means available to get Him freed but at the same time those who sought to curry favour with the Grand Vizier and the Sháh's mother worked to condemn Him. It was at the insistence of the Russian minister, who had worked persistently to establish Bahá'u'lláh's innocence, that 'Aẓím was led into the Síyáh-Chál and, face-to-face with Him, declared that Bahá'u'lláh had played no part in the conspiracy to take the life of the Sh͟áh. 'Aẓím was the last of the Bábís to die in that holocaust. A siyyid, armed with a club, rushed at him and smashed his head, a mob armed with sticks, stones and daggers then fell upon his body.

Finally, the Sh͟áh pronounced that Bahá'u'lláh, along with a number of others, was sentenced to life imprisonment. The reason stated in the court was that His guilt had not been proved.

CHAPTER 8

IN THE HOLY AND SHINING CITY

FEW people kept in the Síyáh-Chál survived for long. A number of the Bábí prisoners died there, their premature deaths brought on by the ghastly conditions they were forced to endure. Bahá'u'lláh was imprisoned there for four agonizing months. In the dark hopelessness of that terrible dungeon, God spoke to Him. Bahá'u'lláh has left us, in His own words, an account of a transcendent, soul-transforming experience which took place in the Síyáh-Chál:

> One night, in a dream, these exalted words were heard on every side: 'Verily, We shall render Thee victorious by Thyself and by Thy Pen. Grieve Thou not for that which hath befallen Thee, neither be Thou afraid, for Thou art in safety. Erelong will God raise up the treasures of the earth – men who will aid Thee through Thyself and through Thy Name, wherewith God hath revived the hearts of such as have recognized Him.[1]

In another Tablet, He wrote:

> While engulfed in tribulations I heard a most wondrous, a most sweet voice, calling above My head. Turning My face, I beheld a Maiden – the embodiment of the remembrance of the name of My Lord – suspended in the air before Me. So rejoiced was she in her very soul that her countenance shone with the ornament of the good-pleasure of God, and her cheeks glowed with the brightness of the All-Merciful. Betwixt earth and heaven she was raising a call which captivated the hearts and minds of men. She was imparting to both My inward and outer being tidings which rejoiced My soul, and the souls of God's honoured servants. Pointing with

her finger unto My head, she addressed all who are in heaven and all who are on earth, saying: 'By God! This is the Best-Beloved of the worlds, and yet ye comprehend not. This is the Beauty of God amongst you, and the power of His sovereignty within you, could ye but understand. This is the Mystery of God and His Treasure, the Cause of God and His glory unto all who are in the kingdoms of Revelation and of creation, if ye be of them that perceive.'[2]

Weighted down by chains, His feet – still sore and festered from the torture of the bastinado – fastened into stocks, breathing the foul air of the dungeon, locked away from the sunlight and warmth, from family and friends in the impenetrable gloom and chill of that prison, Bahá'u'lláh received an intimation from the spiritual realm that He, Himself, was the One of Whom the Báb had spoken and for Whom He had laid down His life. In a letter written much later to the Sháh, Bahá'u'lláh wrote:

O King! I was but a man like others, asleep upon My couch, when lo, the breezes of the All-Glorious were wafted over Me, and taught Me the knowledge of all that hath been. This thing is not from Me, but from One Who is Almighty and All-Knowing. And He bade Me lift up My voice between earth and heaven, and for this there befell Me what hath caused the tears of every man of understanding to flow . . . This is but a leaf which the winds of the will of Thy Lord, the Almighty, the All-Praised, have stirred . . . His all-compelling summons hath reached me, and caused me to speak His praise amidst all people. I was indeed as one dead when His behest was uttered. The hand of the will of Thy Lord, the Compassionate, the Merciful, transformed Me.[3]

With His companions still chained to Him, Bahá'u'lláh experienced an overwhelming outpouring of spiritual illumination as knowledge and strength from the spiritual world were bestowed upon Him. He later wrote:

> During the days I lay in the prison of Ṭihrán, though the galling weight of the chains and the stench-filled air allowed Me but little sleep, still in those infrequent moments of slumber I felt as if something flowed from the crown of My head over My breast, even as a mighty torrent that precipitateth itself upon the earth from the summit of a lofty mountain. Every limb of My body would, as a result, be set afire. At such moments My tongue recited what no man could bear to hear.[4]

It is for this reason that Bahá'u'lláh describes Ṭihrán, the capital city of His homeland, in which so much innocent blood was even then being spilt, as 'the holy and shining city'[5] and states that it is a city destined to become the 'source of the joy of all mankind'.[6]

It was not until Bahá'u'lláh had spent almost four months in the Síyáh-Chál that the persistent efforts of His relatives and friends to secure His release bore fruit. Prince Dolgorouki, who had worked so hard and successfully to establish Bahá'u'lláh's innocence and thereby protect Him from execution, now worked tirelessly to secure His release from prison. It was the documents which had been obtained at the time of 'Aẓím's confession, clearing Bahá'u'lláh of any involvement in the ill-fated conspiracy, that were chiefly responsible for Bahá'u'lláh's release. However, it took three months more of persistent and unrelenting effort before the Grand Vizier was able to gain the Sháh's grudging consent to release Him. The Sháh was not willing that He should be allowed to remain on Persian soil and ordered His banishment.

The royal consent to release from prison obtained, Mírzá Áqá Khán at once sent a trusted emissary, a man named Ḥájí 'Alí, to the Síyáh-Chál with the letters ordering Bahá'u'lláh's release. Ḥájí 'Alí was shaken to the core on witnessing the horror of that place, the filth and squalor, the dripping walls and vermin-infested floor, the chilly darkness and the pitiable condition of the Prisoner. He reportedly cursed his own master, the Grand Vizier, for such shameful treatment of so eminent a citizen.

Bahá'u'lláh's back was bent by the weight of the heavy chains, His neck was brusied and swollen under a heavy steel collar that had cut deep into the skin. He could walk only with difficulty for His feet had been untended since the infliction of the bastinado, four months earlier. He bore, to the end of His life, the scars of that imprisonment.

Moved to pity, Ḥájí 'Alí took off his cloak and offered it to Bahá'u'lláh, entreating Him to wear it at the interview with the Grand Vizier and his ministers, to which He was summoned. Bahá'u'lláh refused his offer, choosing instead to appear before the council in the clothes of a prisoner.

As He entered the council chamber and stood before its members, Mírzá Áqá Khán reprimanded Him severely:

'Had you chosen', he began, 'to take my advice, and had you dissociated yourself from the faith of the Siyyid-i-Báb, you would never have suffered the pains and indignities that have been heaped upon you.'

'Had you, in your turn,' Bahá'u'lláh responded, 'followed my counsels, the affairs of the government would not have reached so critical a stage.'[7]

Taken aback, as he called to mind Bahá'u'lláh's earlier warning to him at the time of the Báb's martyrdom, that 'the flame that has been kindled will blaze forth more fiercely than ever', Mírzá Áqá Khán altered his tone.

'What is it that you advise me now to do?' he asked.

'Command the governors of the realm to cease shedding the blood of the innocent,' Bahá'u'lláh replied, 'to cease plundering their property, to cease dishonouring their women and injuring their children. Let them cease the persecution of the Faith of the Báb; let them abandon the idle hope of wiping out its followers.'[8]

The interview over, the Grand Vizier acted on Bahá'u-

'lláh's advice and sent out these orders but the passions and prejudices already inflamed by the official persecution of the Bábís were so strong and deep that the later orders had only a minimal effect.

Restored to His family, Bahá'u'lláh said little of the ordeals He had endured. Instead, He spoke eloquently of the courage and steadfast faith of His companions who had met their deaths. He told His family nothing of His own mystical experience, but His young daughter, Bahíyyih Khánum, later wrote of those days:

> We saw a new radiance seeming to enfold him like a shining vesture, its significance we were to learn years later. At that time we were only aware of the wonder of it, without understanding, or even being told the details of the sacred event.[9]

No sooner was Bahá'u'lláh released from the prison than an edict was delivered to Him, ordering His immediate banishment from His homeland, permitting Him to choose a place of exile and giving Him just one month in which to prepare His family for departure. As soon as Prince Dolgorouki heard of this edict, he offered Bahá'u'lláh and His family asylum in Russia. He also proferred any assistance necessary to prepare for a winter journey. Bahá'u'lláh courteously declined the offer and chose to move to Baghdád.

It was midwinter in a year of exceptionally severe weather. Bahá'u'lláh had no home, for His houses both in Ṭihrán and Mázindarán lay wrecked and pillaged. He was too weak and ill to help with any preparations for the journey. He moved into the house of His half-brother, Mírzá Riḍá-Qulí, whose wife Maryam nursed Him devotedly, enabling Him to regain a little strength. His two wives, lodged in an obscure corner of the city, hurriedly made what preparations they could, for the government provided nothing for those they banished.

Ásíyih Khánum, assisted by the two devoted African servants – the only servants of all her large household who had not deserted the family in the time of danger – sold a few marriage gifts still in her keeping, some jewels, a few embroidered garments and some other small items for four hundred tumans. With this inadequate sum she bought what supplies she could. Only one relative, her own maternal grandmother, came to visit them during those lonely but hectic days. No one else amongst their numerous relatives and friends dared to associate with them.

On 12 January 1853 Bahá'u'lláh, accompanied by his two wives and their children, together with two of His brothers, Mírzá Músá and Mírzá Muḥammad-Qulí and their dependents, left Ṭihrán by the western gate. The little party was escorted by a representative of the government and an official of the Russian legation.

Bahá'u'lláh was in no fit state of health to embark on a long journey in any weather, let alone a midwinter one. 'Abdu'l-Bahá was only eight years old, Bahíyyih Khánum only six and Ásíyih Khánum was expecting another child. Reluctantly, she had allowed herself to be persuaded to leave the two-year-old Mírzá Mihdí, a delicate child, with her grandmother. This elderly relative was the only soul in all the city who came to bid the exiles a final farewell.

In that freezing winter of 1853, as Bahá'u'lláh and His family floundered towards the high mountain passes of western Persia, in a cold so intense, Bahá'u'lláh later recounted, that it was almost impossible to speak, through ice and snow so abundant that it was hardly possible to move, the fortunes of the infant Bábí Faith dipped to a new low.

Náṣiri'd-Dín Sháh was pleased with himself. He and his

government and the powerful clerics of Persia had, it seemed, succeeded. With the banishment of Bahá'u'lláh from Ṭihrán and from His native land, the Cause of the Báb seemed doomed to extinction. The Sháh's edict of banishment robbed the Bábís of Persia of their one remaining hope of leadership.

The years of persecution and massacre had taken a terrible toll of the Bábí community. The Báb Himself had seen the flower of His following perish before He went to His own death. In January 1851, as the siege of Zanján had become a massacre, Lt. Col Sheil had written of the Bábí movement, 'In every part of Persia his disciples have been crushed or scattered.'[10]

Then, in 1852, the attempted assassination of the Sháh had unleashed a tide of persecution fiercer than any previously experienced. It swept away every one of the leading followers of the Báb, all except for Bahá'u'lláh. While He lay in chains and fetters in the Síyáh-Chál, there was no one to whom the agonized and bewildered Bábís could turn for guidance and reassurance. They were plunged into what seemed an unfathomable abyss of darkness and despair. In Qazvín, the home of Ṭáhirih, four separate groups of Bábís squabbled with each other and occupied themselves with absurd fancies and doctrines. Nabíl-i-A'ẓam, travelling in Khurásán province, where the light of the new Faith had blazed so brightly, wrote, 'The fire of the Cause of God had been well-nigh quenched in every place. I could detect no trace of warmth anywhere.'[11]

In banishing Bahá'u'lláh the Sháh fondly imagined that he had dealt a final blow to the Bábí movement and that he had destroyed any possibility of its revival in his dominion.

But he was mistaken. Though Bahá'u'lláh's body bore the scars of imprisonment, though He was so weak and ill that it seemed scarcely possible that He would survive the rigours of the long journey to Ba<u>gh</u>dád, in His heart there surged an ocean of beauty, might and power. He alone amongst the Báb's grieving followers knew that the darkened embers of their faith would blaze up again, in another land, in unimaginable brightness.

CHAPTER 9
TO BAGHDÁD

THE journey to Baghdád took three months. At night the exiles lodged in caravanserais. One bare room was alloted to each family and no light was allowed at night. They could stay only one night at each caravanserai. Their supplies of food and clothing were inadequate. The food available was so coarse that Bahá'u'lláh could eat little of it. However, He forbade His escort to levy provisions for His party from the impoverished peasantry along the way. He also refused to accept any gifts from the owners and landlords of the villages in which His party lodged.

When they reached a town of any size, Ásíyih Khánum carried her family's clothes to the public bath and there washed them herself. There was, in that bitter winter weather, no way of adequately drying the sodden clothing and her hands, unaccustomed to such work, became cracked and swollen.

At Kirmánsháh, the exiles halted for a few days' rest. Here several Bábís met with Bahá'u'lláh. A number of Shí'ih pilgrims, heading for Karbilá and Najaf, joined Bahá'u'lláh's party in order to make the last stage of their journey in the safety of a group.

Mírzá Yaḥyá was in Kirmánsháh. He was living there in disguise, working as a vendor of shrouds, when the exiles passed through. Hearing of their destination, he expressed a wish to live in Baghdád. He wanted, he explained, to live near Bahá'u'lláh but in his own house so that he could continue to live in disguise and carry on a trade. Bahá'u'lláh gave him some money with which he bought some bales of cotton. He then set out on his own route to Baghdád.

In late March, as the festival of Naw-Rúz drew near, the exiles reached the Ottoman frontier. There they were met by a group of Turkish soldiers who had been assigned to escort them to Baghdád. At the frontier, Bahá'u'lláh sent one of His party ahead with instructions to rent an orchard where they might all rest and celebrate the Naw-Rúz feast. The deep snows of the ice-bound plateau and the perilous mountain passes lay behind them. The springtime streams ran swiftly with the melting snows, trees blossomed, flowers bloomed and birds sang. In an orchard set between palm trees and an orange grove, Bahá'u'lláh and His family rested. On 8 April 1853 they reached Baghdád.

Baghdád, the Abode of Peace, an ancient city – once the capital of the vast 'Abbásid Empire which stretched from Egypt to the borders of China and the seat of the Ottoman caliphate for five hundred years – had enjoyed centuries of splendour, but when Bahá'u'lláh and His party reached its gates it was merely a provincial centre of the crumbling Ottoman Empire with a population of about sixty thousand. Seen from a distance in the 1850s, the outlines of mosques and minarets with graceful spires still looked impressive but the tall brick walls hid a labyrinth of dark, airless and grimy streets and alleyways. The city's two gates, closed from sunset to sunrise, were constantly guarded by soldiers.

The river, however, and the caravan routes across the desert still brought a steady stream of travellers and traders to Baghdád. Camel-trains, mule-trains and an astonishing variety of river craft converged on the city. Baghdád straddles the fast-flowing Tigris, described by Freya Stark, a visitor there in the 1930s as '. . . a noble stream. The only sweet and fresh thoroughfare of the town, not clear water but lion-coloured . . . dyed by the same earth of which the houses and minarets on its banks are built so that all is one tawny harmony.'[1]

The river and the caravan routes brought to Baghdád a multitude of diverse peoples: Bedouin, Kurd, Persian, Jew, Armenian, Chaldean. The city was, traditionally, a centre of espionage where spies, agents, counter-spies and counter-agents met to intrigue, watch and report on each other's activities. There were traders and travellers from as far away as China, India and Africa and Shí'ih pilgrims bound for the holy cities of Najaf and Karbilá. Freya Stark writes of barefoot pilgrims with intense faces and of green-turbanned siyyids in flowing gowns telling their rosaries with grave abstraction.

Near the river banks outside the city lay extensive date groves and fields where beetroot, cucumber and melons were harvested, but at the back of the city, away from the river, the desert encircled the walls. Fig trees, vines and pomegranates grew in small city gardens and in spring the long-legged storks built their swinging nests amongst the city's domes and minarets. Water-buffalo were brought to the river to drink and desert jackals crept nightly to the city walls, there to feast on the refuse tossed over by the city's inhabitants.

The summer temperatures in Baghdád can rise to 140°F, 60°C, in the shade. The blazing desert sun then chokes all vegetation and the desert heat-waves quiver over the city, parching man and beast. The winters too are extreme. Though no snow falls, there are sharp frosts and biting winds that swirl up thick dust-storms. The Baghdád dust Freya Stark described as 'a wicked dust that turns to bloodpoisoning at the slightest opportunity'.[2]

CHAPTER 10

WOES AT THEIR BLACKEST

ON reaching Baghdád, Bahá'u'lláh spent only a few days in the city itself and then moved on to Káẓimayn, a city holy to the Shí'ih Muslims situated some miles north of Baghdád on the west bank of the Tigris. Under its glowing golden cupolas lie the remains of the seventh and the ninth Imáms. Here, the Consul-General of Persia, Mírzá Ibráhím Khán, visited Bahá'u'lláh and advised Him, in view of the fierce devotion of the local people and the visiting pilgrims, to settle in the old quarter of Baghdád which was close to Káẓimayn rather than in Káẓimayn itself. Bahá'u'lláh agreed with this suggestion, and a house was sought for and found. About a month later, Bahá'u'lláh and His family moved back to Baghdád into the house of Ḥájí 'Alí Madad.

Around the time of their arrival in Baghdád, the youngest child of Bahá'u'lláh and Ásíyih Khánum, a son, was born. Ásíyih Khánum was in poor health, her strength diminished by the hardships of the journey. Bahá'u'lláh and Mírzá Músá both helped with the household work. Mírzá Músá sometimes did almost all the household washing himself and he had a special talent for cooking.

When Bahá'u'lláh arrived in Baghdád there was only one Persian Bábí living in the city. In Káẓimayn there was a small handful of believers who had been taught by Ṭáhirih but all of whom now lived in fear of persecution; they did not dare associate with each other in public. The Bábí Faith was regarded as a heresy and if the believers openly spoke of their beliefs they risked losing their lives.

As soon as Bahá'u'lláh arrived in Baghdád, this dwindling

remnant of the Bábí community, reduced both in numbers and moral standing, turned to Him for comfort, reassurance and guidance. They were not disappointed. While imprisoned in the Síyáh-Chál, Bahá'u'lláh had long pondered and meditated on the pitiable condition of the Bábí community and had resolved that His first duty on His release would be 'to arise . . . and undertake, with the utmost vigour, the task of regenerating this people'.[1]

His very presence in the city was balm to the grieving and leaderless Bábí community. Through His words and deeds, He restored to them courage and confidence. Patiently, He began to deepen their limited understanding of the Báb's mission. Furthermore, soon after His arrival in the city He decided to appear in public and, gradually, as He gained the respect of the people, He spoke openly of the Báb's teachings.

About two months after Bahá'u'lláh and His immediate family arrived in Baghdád, Mírzá Yaḥyá reached the city in disguise. Under an assumed name, he worked as a burner of charcoal. At the same time, he attempted to get the Bábís of the area to acknowledge him as their leader. They paid him scant attention. Bahá'u'lláh advised him that, since he had not personally been mentioned in the edict of banishment, he could return to Persia and there render useful service to the friends. Mírzá Yaḥyá chose to remain in Baghdád.

Mírzá Yaḥyá was not a strong character. He was arrogant, lazy, not particularly intelligent and definitely lacking in courage. While living in obscurity, maintaining a strict disguise and never actually making himself available to the other believers, he claimed that Bahá'u'lláh was preventing the rest of the Bábís from acknowledging him, Mírzá Yaḥyá, as the leader of the community. His vanity and arrogant claims were carefully stoked through the subtle prompting of a professed Bábí named Siyyid Muḥammad, who was living in Karbilá.

Siyyid Muḥammad, a former theological student from Iṣfáhán, had moved to Karbilá when he was forced, for some reason, to abandon his studies in Iṣfáhán. In Karbilá he joined the Bábí community but his behaviour at the time of the Báb's martyrdom revealed a singular lack of faith. He was already settled in Karbilá when Bahá'u'lláh visited the city in 1851. The reverent devotion shown to Bahá'u'lláh by the other Bábís during that visit had aroused in him a fierce envy. Bahá'u'lláh's patience and forbearance towards him had served only to inflame a hatred which he had continued to nurse. When Mírzá Yaḥyá arrived in Baghdád, Siyyid Muḥammad found in him the perfect instrument for the furtherance of his own designs. He discovered that he could use Mírzá Yaḥyá as a lever with which to create dissension within the small community and turn the Bábís away from Bahá'u'lláh. Every instance of respect and devotion towards Bahá'u'lláh further inflamed his envy and stirred him to further action.

Into this highly-charged and menacing atmosphere there came a Bábí youth from Káshán named Mírzá Áqá Ján. Mírzá Áqá Ján was neither learned nor wealthy; in Káshán he had earned a living by making soap. One night, in a dream, he had seen the face of the Báb. Soon afterwards he had come across some of the writings of Bahá'u'lláh. Learning that Bahá'u'lláh was in Baghdád, he precipitately left his home in Káshán and made his way to 'Iráq. Arriving in Baghdád, he learnt that Bahá'u'lláh was staying in Karbilá. There he hurried.

Bahá'u'lláh was staying for a few days at the home of one of the Bábís of Karbilá, a certain Ḥájí Mírzá Ḥasan-i-Ḥakím-Báshí, who welcomed the young Bábí from Káshán to his home. On that very night of his arrival in Karbilá, Bahá'u'lláh revealed to Mírzá Áqá Ján a glimpse of the ocean of light that lay within Him. Mírzá Áqá Ján later recounted the events of that memorable night to Nabíl-i-A'ẓam.

As it was summer-time Bahá'u'lláh was in the habit of passing His evenings and of sleeping on the roof of the House. [Áqá Mírzá Muḥammad-Qulí and I sprinkled water on the roof, swept and carpeted it, until He came. He talked to us, had His dinner and retired to rest.] That night, when He had gone to sleep, I, according to His directions, lay down for a brief rest, at a distance of a few feet from Him. No sooner had I risen, and . . . started to offer my prayers, in a corner of the roof which adjoined a wall, than I beheld His blessed Person rise and walk towards me. When He reached me He said: 'You, too, are awake.' Whereupon He began to chant and pace back and forth. How shall I ever describe that voice and the verses it intoned, and His gait, as He strode before me! Methinks, with every step he took and every word He uttered thousands of oceans of light surged before my face, and thousands of worlds of incomparable splendour were unveiled to my eyes, and thousands of suns blazed their light upon me! In the moonlight that streamed upon Him, He thus continued to walk and to chant. Every time He approached me He would pause, and, in a tone so wondrous that no tongue can describe it, would say: 'Hear Me, My son. By God, the True One! This Cause will assuredly be made manifest. Heed thou not the idle talk of the people of the Bayán, who pervert the meaning of every word.' In this manner He continued to walk and chant, and to address me these words until the first streaks of dawn appeared . . . Afterwards I removed His bedding to His room, and, having prepared His tea for Him, was dismissed from His presence.[2]

Mírzá Áqá Ján's soul was afire. He could not hide his intense devotion to Bahá'u'lláh. This blazing love and ardent reverence was instantly detected by Siyyid Muḥammad.

Next there came to Baghdád a learned and highly-respected Bábí named Ḥájí Mírzá Kamálu'd-Dín-i-Naráqí. He came seeking from Mírzá Yaḥyá an explanation of a certain verse in the Qur'án – 'All food was allowed to the children of Israel'. Mírzá Yaḥyá grudgingly consented to his request but produced a trivial and worthless commentary, an affront to the intelligence and learning of the ḥájí. Ḥájí Mírzá Kamálu'd-Dín then turned to Bahá'u'lláh and repeated his request. Bahá'u'lláh wrote for him an exquisite and highly illuminating commentary in which Israel and his children were identified with the Báb and His followers. Ḥájí Mírzá Kamálu'd-Dín found in this text and in the person of Bahá'u'lláh all that his thirsty soul craved. He also recognized Bahá'u'lláh as the One for Whom the Báb had given His life. It was only in deference to Bahá'u'lláh's wishes that he refrained from blazoning far and wide his discovery.

It was not only the reverent devotion of the Bábís that fed Siyyid Muḥammad's jealousy. Steadily the circle of Bahá'u-'lláh's friends and admirers widened. Government officials, even the Governor of Baghdád, began to realize that this Exile was unlike any other who had come from Persia. Those who had been the companions of Siyyid Káẓim sought Him out. Siyyid Muḥammad, consumed with envy, was stirred to ever more subtle scheming. Cunningly, he misrepresented, challenged and criticized Bahá'u'lláh's writings. Through rumours and insinuations, he continually spread doubt and suspicion amongst the Bábís. Bahá'u'lláh, he suggested, was subverting the laws of the Báb. He was, he hinted, usurping the office bestowed by the Báb upon Mírzá Yaḥyá. He even attempted to injure Bahá'u'llah's person, but failed.

The atmosphere of the Bábí community was poisoned. Mutual trust, confidence, unity, none of these could any longer exist. Every effort that Bahá'u'lláh made to alter the rapidly deteriorating situation was fruitless. Woes at their blackest had fallen upon Him. He had escaped from the 'fetters of His foes', He recounted, only to suffer more severely from the 'perfidy of His friends'.

'Oceans of sadness', He wrote at this time in the Tablet of Qullu'ṭ-Ṭa'ám, 'have surged over Me, a drop of which no

Bag͟hdád cafe.

Sar-Galú.

soul could bear to drink. Such is my grief that My soul hath well nigh departed from My body.'[3]

One early morning, between dawn and sunrise, Mírzá Áqa Ján was in the street outside Bahá'u'lláh's house when Bahá'u'lláh emerged from His home. Overwhelming anguish was evident in His features and He spoke in anger.

'These creatures', Bahá'u'lláh pronounced 'are the same creatures who for three thousand years have worshipped idols, and bowed down before the Golden Calf. Now, too, they are fit for nothing better. What relation can there be between this people and Him Who is the Countenance of Glory? What ties can bind them to the One Who is the supreme embodiment of all that is lovable?'[4]

So powerful was the effect of His appearance and His words on Mírzá Áqá Ján that he was unable to move.

'I stood', he later told Nabíl, 'rooted to the spot, lifeless, dried up as a dead tree, ready to fall under the impact of the stunning power of His words.'[5]

Finally, Bahá'u'lláh said: 'Bid them recite: "Is there any Remover of difficulties save God? Say: Praised be God! He is God! All are His servants, and all abide by His bidding!" Tell them to repeat it five hundred times, nay, a thousand times, by day and by night, sleeping and waking, that haply the Countenance of Glory may be unveiled to their eyes, and tiers of light descend upon them.'[6]

Very early on the morning of 10 April 1854, before anyone else in the house was awake, Bahá'u'lláh left Baghdád with one companion. He told no one where He was going.

CHAPTER 11

IN THE WILDERNESS

HE was dressed in the coarse, rough garments of a dervish and took with Him one change of clothing, a kashkúl or alms-bowl and a little food – a small amount of rice and some coarse bread. His only companion was a Muslim named Abu'l-Qásim from Hamadán. Together, they travelled over two hundred miles to the north of Baghdád, to the small town of Sulaymáníyyih which lies beneath a barren range in the foothills of the Zagros mountains.

Kurdistán, the homeland of the Kurdish peoples, spills across the northern Zagros. The Kurds, a sturdy and warlike people, have a distinctive language, culture and outlook on life. They are Sunní Muslims and have nursed an age-long hostility to their Persian Shi'ih neighbours, regarding them as deviators from the true Faith.

The majority of the inhabitants of Sulaymáníyyih, pursued a semi-nomadic existence. In the spring, when fresh grass, gentians and anemones carpet the hills, most of the townspeople moved out of the town to live through the summer months in their black tents, returning only to Sulaymáníyyih with the cold winter weather.

When they reached Sulaymáníyyih, Bahá'u'lláh gave Abu'l-Qásim a sum of money, requesting Him to support himself as a trader. He then moved on to a mountain called Sar Galú, three days' journey from the nearest human habitation. So remote was the spot that the local farmers visted the area only twice a year, at seed-time and harvest.

In that lonely spot, Bahá'u'lláh found the solitude He sought. Taking the name of Darvísh Muḥammad-i-Íráni,

He lived there for almost two years as a hermit, spending His days, and often His nights also, in prayer and meditation. In the worst weather, He found rough shelter in a cave and also in a primitive stone shelter built by the local farmers near the summit of the mountain.

'The birds of the air', He later wrote of that period, 'were My companions and the beasts of the field My associates.'[1] 'For two years or rather less I shunned all else but God, and closed Mine eyes to all except Him, that haply the fire of hatred may die down and the heat of jealousy abate'.[2] 'The one object of Our retirement was to avoid becoming a subject of discord among the faithful, a source of disturbance unto Our companions, the means of injury to any soul, or the cause of sorrow to any heart.'[3]

He had realized that the deep divisions within the small Bábí community would not heal while He remained in Baghdád. The intensity of pain and anguish which He experienced at the disunity of the Bábís led Him to turn towards His Creator in ardent prayer and supplication:

> From Our eyes there rained tears of anguish, and in Our bleeding heart there surged an ocean of agonizing pain. Many a night We had no food for sustenance, and many a day Our body found no rest. By Him Who hath My being between His hands! notwithstanding these showers of afflictions and unceasing calamities, Our soul was wrapt in blissful joy, and Our whole being evinced an ineffable gladness. For in Our solitude We were unaware of the harm or benefit, the health or ailment, of any soul. Alone, We communed with Our spirit, oblivious of the world and all that is therein.[4]

It was during this lonely sojourn in Kurdistán that Bahá'u'lláh revealed the short prayer which begins:

> Create in me a pure heart, O my God, and renew a tranquil conscience within me, O my Hope! Through the spirit of

> power confirm Thou me in Thy Cause, O my Best-Beloved, and by the light of Thy glory reveal unto me Thy path, O Thou the Goal of my desire![5]

The food He ate was of the simplest, for the most part coarse bread with a little cheese. Occasionally, He would walk down to Sulaymáníyyih to obtain essential supplies and to visit the public bath. On these visits, He stayed at the theological seminary. Sometimes Abu'l-Qásim took a few provisions out to Him.

In spite of His seclusion, the very few people He came in contact with glimpsed something of His remarkable qualities. His kindness to the few local people He encountered led them to love Him; the wisdom of the few words He spoke caused them to revere Him.

He had told no one in His family where He was going nor when or even if He would return. He had, however, before His departure, offered Mírzá Yaḥyá the hospitality of His own home and had counselled Ásíyih Khánum and her children and His two faithful brothers, Mírzá Músá and Mírzá Muḥammad-Qulí, to see to Mírzá Yaḥyá's needs and to do everything that they could to make him comfortable.

Grieving at His absence, they strove to satisfy a difficult house guest. Mírzá Yaḥyá was so terrified of being arrested that he kept the door of the house locked and flew into a rage whenever anyone opened it. He would not allow any member of the household to go out into the streets, not even to visit the public bath, nor would he allow anyone into the house to help with the heavy household tasks. When the youngest child of Bahá'u'lláh and Ásíyih Khánum, born around the time of their arrival in Baghdád, fell ill, Mírzá Yaḥyá forbade Ásíyih Khánum to summon a doctor or even a neighbour. When the baby died, he forbade them to leave the house for the burial nor would he allow anyone in to prepare the body for interment. The tiny body was handed over to a stranger at the door and Ásíyih Khánum never learnt where he was buried.

Mírzá Yaḥyá would not meet with the rest of the Bábís. He even forbade them to mention the name of the street where he lived. But, while closeted in the house, he managed, through a constant stream of letters to a small handful of followers, to further aggravate the existing dissension and disunity.

As a result of the absence of leadership, in the two years of Bahá'u'lláh's absence from Baghdád, no less than twenty-five Bábís claimed to be 'Him Whom God shall make manifest'. Some did so simply because they knew themselves to be more capable than Mírzá Yaḥyá. Dayyán, a distinguished follower of the Báb in Ádharbáyján, was one of those who made such a claim. In response, Mírzá Yaḥyá at once sent one of his supporters to Ádharbáyján with orders to murder Dayyán. The assassin failed only because Dayyán had left his home town and was on his way to Baghdád.

Mírzá Yaḥyá persuaded Mírzá Áqá Ján to travel all the way to Núr and there await an opportunity to kill the Sháh. In Baghdád itself, he ordered the murder of a fervent admirer of Dayyán, a man named Mírzá 'Alí-Akbar, a cousin of the Báb.

The Bábí community was on the brink of total and irreparable disintegration. In Karbilá, Siyyid Muḥammad allowed and even encouraged the band of ruffians that had gathered about him to abuse, molest and steal from the wealthy pilgrims visiting the holy shrines. His followers snatched away the turbans and shoes of the pilgrims and even stole divans and candles from inside the shrine itself and drinking cups from the public fountains. The reputation of the Bábís sank so low in those days that the few Bábís hardly dared show their faces on the street. When they did so, the Kurds and Persians openly abused them and their Faith. A few Bábís who had travelled, with great difficulty, all the way from Persia to Baghdád in search of comfort and assurance, found neither. Mírzá Yaḥyá categorically refused to see them.

During this period, Ásíyih Khánum and Mírzá Músá moved their families into a larger house. Mírzá Yaḥyá was too frightened of being seen to make the move with them. He insisted on occupying a smaller house behind theirs but he continued to depend on them for his food and other provisions.

While the condition of the Bábí community in Baghdád went from bad to worse, Bahá'u'lláh continued to live alone at Sar-Galú. When he visited Sulaymáníyyih, He observed a strict silence and reserve. It was only because He one day helped a young student who waited on Him at the theological seminary with his lesson that a sample of His exquisite calligraphy was seen there. Students and teachers alike at once wished to know more about the hermit who came and went so quietly.

A certain shaykh of Sulaymáníyyih who owned some property near Sar-Galú was led, through the influence of a dream he had of the Prophet Muḥammad, to interview the solitary dervish. Once this contact was established, word spread rapidly. A prominent Ṣúfí leader, Shaykh Ismá'íl, sought Bahá'u'lláh's presence. After repeated requests, he persuaded Bahá'u'lláh to leave the mountain and move into Sulaymáníyyih. There He won the hearts of all who came into His presence.

At the seminary where He now lived, a group of the most eminent doctors and their most distinguished students asked Bahá'u'lláh to elucidate for them the intricacies of a certain book written by the great mystic writer of Muslim Spain, the Andalusian Shaykh Muḥyí'd-Din Ibnu'l-'Arabí. Bahá'u'lláh replied that He had never read the book but He agreed to their request. Each day a page of this book was read aloud in His presence. Each day Bahá'u'lláh resolved the difficulties they had encountered in understanding it. He clarified its obscure passages, helped them to see into the mind of its author and to understand his motive in writing it. In several instances He questioned the soundness of certain of the writer's views and offered a convincing alternative presentation of the issues.

Astonished by the depth of Bahá'u'lláh's understanding, the scholars now made a further request.

'No one among the mystics, the wise, and the learned', they stated, 'has hitherto proved himself capable of writing a poem in a rhyme and metre identical with that of the longer of the two odes, entitled Qaṣídiy-i-Tá'íyyih composed by Ibn-i-Fárid. We beg you to write for us a poem in that same metre and rhyme.'[6] Bahá'u'lláh acceded to this request also and wrote for them a poem of two thousand verses in the exact rhyme and metre requested. From these He selected a hundred and twenty-seven verses which he permitted them to keep. Bahá'u'lláh's poem, they all agreed, far surpassed in power and beauty the ode of the celebrated Ibn-i-Fárid.

This event stimulated intense interest and drew into the presence of Bahá'u'lláh increasing numbers of eminent and learned men. He kept to the dress of a dervish, His food was that of the poor but He was revered and loved by all with whom He came in contact and news of the holy and learned dervish reached even to Ba<u>gh</u>dád.

'In a short time', 'Abdu'l-Bahá later wrote, 'Kurdistán was magnetized with His love . . . An atmosphere of majesty haloed Him as the sun at midday.'[7]

These two years in the wilderness were, Bahá'u'lláh Himself wrote, 'the most perfect and conclusive evidence' of the truth of His Revelation.[8]

Around this time, nearly two years after Bahá'u'lláh and Abu'l-Qásim had left Ba<u>gh</u>dád, word reached the city that Abu'l-Qásim had been robbed by thieves on the Persian border and left for dead. Mortally hurt, he was able only to say to his rescuers that he was Abu'l-Qásim, a native of Hamadán, and that all that he carried belonged to Darvísh Muḥammad-i-Írání.

All this time Bahá'u'lláh's family had anxiously sought for news of Him. When they heard of Abu'l-Qásim's death and that he had left Baghdád at the same time as Bahá'u'lláh, they realized that the revered Darvísh-i-Írání could be none other than Bahá'u'lláh. At the insistence of 'Abdu'l-Bahá and Mírzá Musá, Shaykh Sulṭán and one other Bábí companion set out for Sulaymáníyyih. They carried with them letters detailing the sad condition of the community and begging Bahá'u'lláh to return. Mírzá Yaḥyá, aware that matters were slipping rapidly beyond his control, had also written, urgently pleading with Bahá'u'lláh to return.

Bahá'u'lláh responded to these appeals. In slow stages, He retraced His steps towards Baghdád, directing His admirers in Kurdistán, desolate at His departure, to seek Him in Baghdád in the house of Mírzá Músá, the Persian. Those few days of the journey south were, He told Shaykh Sulṭán, 'the only days of peace and tranquillity' left to Him, 'days which', He said, 'will never again fall to My lot.'[9]

'But for My recognition', Bahá'u'lláh admitted to Shaykh Sulṭán, 'of the fact that the blessed Cause of the Primal Point was on the verge of being completely obliterated, and all the sacred blood poured out in the path of God would have been shed in vain, I would in no wise have consented to return to the people of the Bayán, and would have abandoned them to the worship of the idols their imaginations had fashioned.'[10]

CHAPTER 12

A RISING SPLENDOUR

STILL dressed in the garments of a dervish, Bahá'u'lláh entered the city. His family's joy at His return was unbounded. Bahíyyih Khánum wrote of those final, long days of waiting and anticipation:

> Hope now brought its brilliance into the dark shadow of our anxiety, which had saddened our lives for two years. . . My mother had made a coat for him out of some pieces of precious Persian stuff which she had carefully kept for the purpose out of the remains of her marriage treasures. It was now ready for him to put on.
>
> At last! At last! As my mother, my brother, and I sat in a breathless state of expectancy, we heard a step. It was a dervish. Through the disguise we saw the light of our beloved one's presence!
>
> Our joy cannot be described as we clung to him.[1]

At the time of Bahá'u'lláh's return there were no more than thirty to forty Bábís in Baghdád. Some of these had been led astray by Mírzá Yaḥyá and Siyyid Muḥammad. Of the remainder, all were confused and demoralized. The Bábí community was on the verge of extinction. So low had it sunk in the esteem of the people of Baghdád that its members were abused and insulted when they appeared on the streets and in the bazaars.

'We found', Bahá'u'lláh lamented, 'no more than a handful of souls, faint and dispirited, nay utterly lost and dead. The Cause of God had ceased to be on any one's lips, nor was any heart receptive to its message.'[2]

Plunged into intense grief on witnessing the condition of

His fellow-believers, for some time Bahá'u'lláh scarcely left His house. To a brimming cup of sorrow was added a fresh, bitter blow. Dayyán, whom Mírzá Yaḥyá had attempted to have put to death in Ádharbáyján, had reached Baghdád in Bahá'u'lláh's absence and was still in the city at His return. As soon as he could, he gained Bahá'u'lláh's presence. There he renounced all claims to leadership of the Bábí community. Mírzá Yaḥyá, however, was not to be deflected. Still driven by a wild jealousy, he ordered one of his followers to bring about Dayyán's death. At a lonely spot on the road between Baghdád and Káẓimayn, this gifted and distinguished follower of the Báb was murdered.

The Bábís, already reviled as thieves and robbers, could fall no lower. The shamed and fractured community was floundering in an extremity of despair and confusion. Bahá'u'lláh wrote:

> . . . what showers of continuous sorrows, their words and deeds have caused to rain upon Our soul! Amidst them all, We stand, life in hand, wholly resigned to His will; that perchance, through God's loving-kindness and His grace, this revealed and manifest Letter may lay down His life as a sacrifice in the path of the Primal Point, the most exalted Word.[3]

The task of regenerating the Bábí community was daunting but Bahá'u'lláh undertook it. Gradually, by the force of example, through His spoken and written words, with patience and loving-kindness, He began to shepherd the Bábís out of their pit of shame. They gathered at His house several times a day. There He deepened their understanding of the Cause to which they were committed, restored to them a sense of purpose and direction and at the same time raised their moral and ethical standards above the highest principles which the Báb Himself had laid down. Even He could not, however, always hold in check the impetuous hotheads amongst the believers. Some of the Bábís fell upon two of the followers of Mírzá Yaḥyá, killing them both. Others answered the Shí'ihs who taunted them with violence. Bahá'u'lláh condemned these actions but could not always prevent them. They caused Him great anguish.

The principles and standards of behaviour which Bahá'u-'lláh imparted to the few dozen Bábís gathered at that time in the neighbourhood of Baghdád are the same as those towards which Bahá'ís all over the world strive today. Shoghi Effendi has summarized them in these words:

> The dissociation . . . from every form of political activity and from all secret associations and factions; the emphasis placed on the principle of non-violence; the necessity of strict obedience to established authority; the ban imposed on all forms of sedition, on back-biting, retaliation, and dispute; the stress laid on godliness, kindliness, humility and piety, on honesty and truthfulness, chastity and fidelity, on justice, toleration, sociability, amity and concord, on the acquisition of arts and sciences, on self-sacrifice and detachment, on patience, steadfastness and resignation to the will of God – all these constitute the salient features of a code of ethical conduct to which the books, treatises and epistles, revealed during those years, by the indefatigable pen of Bahá'u'lláh, unmistakably bear witness.[4]

Bahá'u'lláh spent several hours each day in the various coffee houses of the city. There He taught the Cause of the Báb openly. Such a venture carried risk for there were many in the city who were openly hostile to the Faith. Bahá'u'lláh never avoided their presence. Many came to admire and respect Him even though they did not become Bábís. At one time a hostile group of Kurdish people came to His home, intent on harming Him. He opened His doors to them and disarmed them of their evil intent with hospitality and loving-kindness.

During His absence in Kurdistán, a number of prominent Bábís, some of whom had made claims to the leadership of the Bábí community, had reached Baghdád. One by one, those stalwart servants of the Báb, who had suffered so greatly in His cause and who had made their own claims to leadership solely as a result of the glaring deficiencies of Mírzá Yaḥyá's leadership, entered Bahá'u'lláh's presence. There they renounced their own claims and sought His forgiveness.

Very soon after Bahá'u'lláh's return to Baghdád His devoted admirers in Kurdistán began to arrive in the city seeking Him. The appearance of prominent Kurdish 'ulamá and Ṣúfí leaders seeking reverently for 'Darvísh Muḥammad' at 'the house of Mírzá Músá, the Bábí' aroused considerable curiosity and wonder. The local religious leaders, government officials, notables and many of the distinguished Persians living in the city wondered what it was that they were missing. They, along with poets, mystics and seekers from Muslim, Jewish and Christian backgrounds, all sought Bahá'u'lláh's presence and, once admitted, returned again and again.

'I know not how to explain it,' said one of these visitors, a Persian prince, 'were all the sorrows of the world to be crowded into my heart they would, I feel, all vanish, when in the presence of Bahá'u'lláh. It is as if I had entered Paradise itself.'[5]

If strangers drew such comfort, the joy of the local Bábís and of the Bábí pilgrims, arriving in ever-increasing numbers from Persia to seek His presence, can scarcely be imagined.

> So inebriated, so carried away was every one by the sweet savours of the Morn of Divine Revelation that, methinks, out of every thorn sprang forth heaps of blossoms, and every seed yielded innumerable harvests.[6]

So intoxicated were those who had quaffed from the cup of Bahá'u'lláh's presence, that in their eyes the palaces of kings appeared more ephemeral than a spider's web . . . Many a night no less than ten persons subsisted on no more than a pennyworth of dates. No one knew to whom actually belonged the shoes, the cloaks, or the robes that were to be found in their houses . . . Their own names they had forgotten, their hearts were emptied of aught else except adoration for their Beloved . . . O, for the joy of those days, and the gladness and wonder of those hours![7]

Already in the two years before He left for Kurdistán, Bahá'u'lláh's home had become a haven and refuge for the poor and distressed of the district of Kharkh in which He lived. On His return, the numbers seeking comfort, assistance and counsel steadily increased. On the orphaned, the disabled, the grieving and the oppressed, Bahá'u'lláh showered his loving-kindness. As friends and relatives in Persia recovered some of the proceeds from the sale of His properties and possessions, He was able to extend His generosity further. People of all classes, rich and poor, learned and illiterate, were drawn to Him. One such was an elderly woman, short of stature and bent with age. She lived in an impoverished area of the city through which Bahá'u'lláh walked on His way to one of the city's coffee houses. Every day she waited outside her home to see Him pass. Bahá'u'lláh was unfailingly kind to her and in gratitude she wished to kiss His hands, according to the custom of the time. This Bahá'u'lláh would not allow but whenever she wished to kiss His cheek He would bend down so that she might reach Him. 'Because I love this old woman so much,' He said, 'she also loves Me.'[8]

Bahá'u'lláh and His family lived in the utmost simplicity and austerity. At one time, while in 'Iráq, He had only one shirt which 'would be washed, dried and worn again'.[9] Nabíl relates that during this time he and two companions lived in a room devoid of furniture. On entering it one day, Bahá'u'lláh remarked: 'Its emptiness pleases Me. In My estimation it is preferable to many a spacious palace, inasmuch as the beloved of God are occupied in it with the remembrance of the Incomparable Friend, with hearts that are wholly emptied of the dross of this world.'[10]

In just a few years, through Bahá'u'lláh's guidance, the small Bábí community of Baghdád was recreated, renewed, reborn. From the depths of ignominy and shame, the Bábís became renowned through the city for their honesty and upright conduct. Several of the believers opened shops and their singular honesty attracted buyers and raised the prestige of the Bábí community.

The effects of Bahá'u'lláh's guidance were not confined to 'Iráq. In 1853, the year of His arrival in Baghdád, Shaykh Salmán travelled to 'Iráq in order to act as Bahá'u'lláh's courier. Bringing letters from Persia, he returned with Tablets for the believers, a service he was to continue for the rest of his life.

Of this period Bahá'u'lláh wrote,

> By the aid of God and His divine grace and mercy, We revealed, as a copious rain, Our verses, and sent them to various parts of the world. We exhorted all men, and particularly this people, through Our wise counsels and loving admonitions, and forbade them to engage in sedition, quarrels, disputes or conflict. As a result of this, and by the grace of God, waywardness and folly were changed into piety and understanding, and weapons of war converted into instruments of peace.[11]

While walking on the banks of the Tigris, Bahá'u'lláh revealed *The Hidden Words*, a small book which Shoghi Effendi describes as 'dynamic spiritual leaven cast into the life of the world for the reorientation of the minds of men, the edification of their souls and the rectification of their conduct'.[12]

In response to the questions of a Ṣúfí leader, Bahá'u'lláh revealed His mystical work *The Seven Valleys* in which He traces the journey of the soul of a seeker towards the knowledge and love of God. In answer to questions put to Him by Ḥájí Mírzá Siyyid Muḥammad, a maternal uncle of the Báb who had not, at that point, accepted his nephew's Cause, Bahá'u'lláh revealed His foremost theological work, the *Kitáb-i-Íqán* (*The Book of Certitude*). This, Shoghi Effendi has described as a 'unique repository of inestimable treasures' which 'by sweeping away the age-long barriers that have so insurmountably separated the great religions of the world, has laid down a broad and unassailable foundation for the complete and permanent reconciliation of their followers'.[13]

The volume of the writings Bahá'u'lláh revealed while in Baghdád was enormous but by His express order, hundreds of thousands of verses, written mostly in His own hand, were washed off the paper and the paper thrown into the river. Mírzá Áqá Ján was given this unenviable task.

'Finding me reluctant to execute His orders,' he told Nabíl, 'Bahá'u'lláh would reassure me saying: "None is to be found at this time worthy to hear these melodies" . . . Not once, or twice, but innumerable times, was I commanded to repeat this act.'[14]

Those who witnessed Bahá'u'lláh revealing His letters, Tablets and epistles needed no further proof of His mission. Muḥammad Karím, a Bábí of Shíráz, wrote,

> I bear witness that the verses revealed by Bahá'u'lláh were superior, in the rapidity with which they were penned, in the ease with which they flowed, in their lucidity, their profundity and sweetness to those which I, myself, saw pour from the pen of the Báb when in His presence. Had Bahá'u'lláh no other claim to greatness, this were sufficient, in the eyes of the world and its people, that He produced such verses as have streamed this day from His pen.[15]

Within just a few years of Bahá'u'lláh's return from Sulaymáníyyih, the condition of the Bábí community was transformed and Bahá'u'lláh Himself was held in the highest esteem. A reaction from the forces of orthodoxy was inevitable. It was triggered by a scheming and strong-willed Shí'ih priest named Shaykh 'Abdu'l-Ḥusayn, who arrived in Karbilá in 1858. He had come armed with a mandate from the Sháh authorizing him to supervise the repair of the holy sites of Karbilá. In fact, the Grand Vizier had found him so troublesome that he had prevailed on the Sháh to send him to Karbilá, out of the way. Shaykh 'Abdu'l-Ḥusayn, a proud and ambitious man, at once became jealous of Bahá'u'lláh. He tried, by every means in his power, to injure His reputation. In 1860 he acquired a willing ally in the newly-appointed Persian Consul-General to Baghdád, Mírzá Buzurg Khán, a self-seeking individual of meagre intellect and few morals.

The first step these two men attempted, by means of slander, was to obtain an order for the return of Bahá'u'lláh and His family to Persia. This failed. Shaykh 'Abdu'l-Ḥusayn then began to stir up a credulous populace by relating to them dreams of his own invention which he interpreted as representing warnings of the danger to true believers posed by the Bábí community. An interview was arranged for him to meet with Bahá'u'lláh but he had not the courage to appear at the appointed time. Mírzá Buzurg Khán, in his turn, stirred up the passions of the unruly mob elements of the city. His aim was to precipitate a public affront to Bahá'u'lláh which would, he hoped, provoke a retaliatory act by one of the Bábís. Such an act of violence committed by a Bábí would provide him with grounds for demanding extradition. This attempt also failed. Bahá'u'lláh continued to frequent the streets and the coffee houses, often unescorted. Instead of avoiding those who sought to abuse Him, He confronted them and joked with them. His would-be molesters soon abandoned any idea of abusing Him.

Mírzá Buzurg Khán then hired an assassin, gave him money, a horse and two pistols and ordered him to kill Bahá'u'lláh. This hired killer, a notorious ruffian named Riḍá Turk, made two attempts. First he managed to enter the public bath while Bahá'u'lláh was visiting it without being seen by the vigilant Bábís. In the inner chamber of the bath, armed with a pistol which he had concealed under his cloak, he encountered Bahá'u'lláh but found that he had not the courage to use the pistol. Then he lay in wait for Bahá'u'lláh, pistol in hand, in the crowded streets. Bahá'u'lláh appeared in company with His brother Mírzá Músá. As soon as he saw Bahá'u'lláh, Riḍá Turk became so confused and perplexed that he dropped the pistol. As he himself recounted in later years, he was unable even to bend down and pick it up. 'Pick up his pistol and give it to him,' Bahá'u'lláh said to Mírzá Músá as they drew level with Riḍá Turk, 'and show him the way to his house; he seems to have lost his way.'[16]

Shaykh 'Abdu'l-Ḥusayn now tried a new tack. He could, he assured Mírzá Buzurg Khán, arrange for him to be appointed a minister of the Sháh, if only he, Mírzá Buzurg Khán, could succeed in arranging for Bahá'u'lláh to be recalled to Ṭihrán and thrown into prison again. Shaykh 'Abdu'l-Ḥusayn himself wrote a stream of lengthy reports to the Persian court vilifying Bahá'u'lláh. Bahá'u'lláh had, he wrote, won the allegiance of the nomadic tribes of 'Iráq. He was capable of mustering a hundred thousand armed men. He was plotting a rebellion against the Sháh.

The authorities in Ṭihrán succumbed to these pressures and issued a mandate giving Shaykh 'Abdu'l-Ḥusayn full powers to deal with this matter and calling on the Persian religious leaders and civil officers in 'Iráq to support his efforts. Shaykh 'Abdu'l-Ḥusayn at once forwarded this mandate to the religious leaders of Najaf and Karbilá and asked them to call a meeting in Káẓimayn, where he lived. Many Persian shaykhs, mullás and mujtahids responded instantly for they saw in this matter an opportunity to gain favour in Ṭihrán. Once informed, at the meeting, of the supposed threat to Islám they determined to declare a holy war and to exterminate the Bábís. They immediately sought to obtain the assent to their plans of the leading mujtahid of the holy cities, the learned and highly respected Shaykh Murtaḍáy-i-Anṣárí, summoning him from Karbilá with a message that the welfare of the Faith of Islám was threatened. When he found out what was intended, the Shaykh held himself apart from the gathering. He had not, he said, personally investigated the matter and would not, therefore, intervene. He sent a message to Bahá'u'lláh, the gist of which was 'I did not know; had I done so, I would not have come. Now I will pray for you.'[17] He returned to Najaf.

Deprived of the opportunity of waging holy war against the Bábís, the assembled clerics decided to send an emissary to Bahá'u'lláh with a list of questions which, they said, demanded elucidation. The envoy they chose was a wise and devout man, a certain Ḥájí Mullá Ḥasan-i-'Amú, widely respected for his integrity. When all the questions had been answered to his complete satisfaction, the Ḥájí put forward a further request. He asked Bahá'u'lláh, as a proof of His mission, to perform a miracle. This, he stated, would fully satisfy all.

Bahá'u'lláh replied,

> Although you have no right to ask this, for God should test His creatures and they should not test God, still I allow and accept this request . . . The 'ulamás must assemble, and, with one accord, choose one miracle, and write that, after the performance of this miracle they will no longer entertain doubts about Me, and that all will acknowledge and confess the truth of My Cause. Let them seal this paper, and bring it

> to Me. This must be the accepted criterion: if the miracle is performed, no doubt will remain for them; and if not, We shall be convicted of imposture.[18]

Delighted with this answer, Ḥájí Mullá Ḥasan hurried back to the divines. Three days later he sent word that the assembled clerics had been unable to arrive at a decision and had decided to drop their request.

'We have,' Bahá'u'lláh is said to have stated on hearing of this, 'through this all-satisfying, all-embracing message which We sent, revealed and vindicated the miracles of all the Prophets, inasmuch as We left the choice to the 'ulamás themselves, undertaking to reveal whatever they would decide upon.'[19]

Bahá'u'lláh would, at any time that he was in 'Iráq, have met with the divines of Persia who lived in that country. He wrote,

> For twelve years We tarried in Baghdád. Much as We desired that a large gathering of divines and fair-minded men be convened, so that truth might be distinguished from falsehood, and be fully demonstrated, no action was taken.[20]

None of the religious leaders of the city ever dared to meet with Him.

During these months of intrigue and danger, Bahá'u'lláh never once hid Himself or contemplated an escape from Baghdád but rather went about openly as He had always done. At some point during these years, Colonel Sir Arnold Burrows Kemball, the British Consul-General in the city, offered Bahá'u'lláh the protection of British citizenship. He could, he said, arrange for Bahá'u'lláh and His family to move to India or to any other place in the British Empire agreeable to Him. Bahá'u'lláh thanked him but declined the offer. During his last year in Baghdád, the new Governor, Námiq Páshá, impressed by the respect and veneration paid to this Persian exile, visited Bahá'u'lláh. He too, became a sincere admirer. When the hostility of the 'ulamá rose to fever pitch, Bahá'u'lláh decided that His fellow exiles should apply for Turkish passports. Námiq Páshá gladly granted this request. Two by two, over a period of three weeks, the Bábís went through the necessary formalities and obtained Turkish papers.

Shaykh 'Abdu'l-Ḥusayn and Mírzá Buzurg Khán were stunned when they heard this news for now they could not get the exiles extradited to Persia. In 1862 Mírzá Buzurg Khán was recalled to Ṭihrán where he continued to work for the removal of Bahá'u'lláh from Baghdád.

At the same time, in Constantinople, the Sháh's ambassador to the Ottoman court was steadily working to the same end. Sulṭán 'Abdu'l-Majíd, greatly impressed by the accounts of Bahá'u'lláh sent to him by a succession of governors, consistently refused to consider the removal of Bahá'u'lláh from Baghdád but in 1861 the Sulṭán died and was succeeded by Sulṭán 'Abdu'l-'Azíz. So persistent were the pressures then exerted for Bahá'u'lláh's removal from Baghdád that the ministers of the new Sulṭán finally gave way and ordered Námiq Páshá to invite Bahá'u'lláh to visit Constantinople.

Námiq Páshá was so unwilling to carry out this order that the Turkish Grand Vizier sent him five successive commands over a period of three months before he responded. In late March 1863 Bahá'u'lláh received a message from the Governor requesting Him to visit his official quarter. Bahá'u'lláh replied that He had never set foot there but that He would meet the Governor in a nearby mosque. Throughout His years of exile in 'Iráq, Bahá'u'lláh had never been to any government offices nor, as was the custom of other Persian exiles, had He visited the houses of any Ottoman officials or city leaders. The Governor agreed to His request but at the last moment backed out of the interview and sent his deputy instead. Bahá'u'lláh, attended by one young companion, attended the mosque and there received an invitation to proceed to Constantinople. He accepted the invitation.

The Bábís were overwhelmed by the news, particularly when they understood that Bahá'u'lláh intended to go alone, without even His family. Some resolved to commit suicide rather than be parted from Him. But then Námiq Páshá courteously expressed the hope that His family, His brothers and a number of His companions would go with Him. He offered Bahá'u'lláh a sum of money for the expenses of the journey which Bahá'u'lláh declined but, at the Governor's insistence, took and spent on the poor of the city the same day.

Mírzá Buzurg Khán and Shaykh 'Abdu'l-Ḥusayn saw their schemes brought to nothing. Marked consideration, respect and reverence were paid to the departing exiles.

As April progressed, Bahá'u'lláh showered upon the Bábís of Baghdád His comfort and counsel. For each one of them, men, women and children, He wrote a special Tablet. He met with them in their homes and through His firm and loving words instilled in them hope and confidence. The news of His imminent departure spread rapidly through Baghdád and the neighbouring towns. So great was the throng of visitors who streamed to His home that His family was quite unable to get on with their preparations for the journey. Najíb Páshá, a notable of the city and a fervent admirer of Bahá'u'lláh, hearing of this, offered Bahá'u'lláh the use of a beautiful garden he owned just across the river from Bahá'u'lláh's house.

On 22 April Bahá'u'lláh left His home in Baghdád for the last time. As He appeared in the courtyard of His house, His ardent followers loudly lamented His departure. For some time He stood there comforting them and He promised to receive each of them in the garden later. As He emerged into the street, the crowd surged towards Him. Some threw themselves at His feet, others strained forwards for a last glimpse of His face, others stood hoping for a touch from His hands as He passed. A noble Persian lady, not herself a believer, pushed through the crowd and, with a gesture of sacrifice, threw her child at His feet.

Wearing, for the first time, a táj – a tall, embroidered, felt hat – He walked to the river along streets crowded with well-wishers, rich and poor, learned and illiterate, Muslim, Christian and Jew, all lamenting His departure. As he walked He gave alms to the poor and spoke words of comfort to all. A Sunní leader watching Him pass was seen to weep for his own people, suddenly bereft of such a counsellor.

As Bahá'u'lláh approached the river bank and stepped into the small boat that was to carry Him across the Tigris, a great throng of people pressed close behind Him, unwilling to be parted from His presence. Just before He got into the boat in which He was to cross the river, He addressed these words to the small band of His companions who surrounded Him.

> O My companions, I entrust to your keeping this city of Baghdád, in the state ye now behold it, when from the eyes of friends and strangers alike, crowding its housetops, its streets and markets, tears like the rain of spring are flowing down, and I depart. With you it now rests to watch lest your deeds and conduct dim the flame of love that gloweth within the breasts of its inhabitants.[21]

CHAPTER 13

THE DIVINE SPRINGTIME

TOGETHER with three of His sons, 'Abdu'l-Bahá, Mírzá Mihdí and Muḥammad-'Alí, aged eighteen, fourteen and ten, and His amanuensis, Mírzá Áqá Ján, Bahá'u'lláh was rowed across the fast-flowing river. It was springtime, the loveliest season in Baghdád. Soon would come the searing heat of summer but in late April birds sang and flowers and trees blossomed, filling the air with their fragrance. Bahá'u'lláh's companions had raised His tent and five or six other tents in the garden of Najíb Páshá on the eastern bank of the Tigris. As Bahá'u'lláh entered the garden, the call to afternoon prayer resounded through the flower-filled avenues.

Upon His arrival in the garden of Najíb Páshá on 22 April 1863, Bahá'u'lláh revealed to a small group of His companions that He was the One Whose coming the Báb had foretold, the Holy One Whom they awaited, He Whom God would make manifest. For this reason the garden of Najíb Páshá is called the Garden of Riḍván, the Garden of Paradise, and the twelve days Bahá'u'lláh and His companions spent there are celebrated by Bahá'ís as the Festival of Riḍván, the holiest time in the Bahá'í year. There is no eye-witness account of this momentous declaration available but the words of Bahá'u'lláh in the Riḍván Tablet shed over us the sweet and joyous fragrance of those soul-stirring days:

> This is the Day whereon the true servants of God partake of the life-giving waters of reunion, the Day whereon those that are nigh unto Him are able to drink of the soft-flowing river of immortality, and they who believe in His unity, the wine of

His Presence, through their recognition of Him Who is the Highest and Last End of all . . .

The Best-Beloved is come. In His right hand is the sealed Wine of His name. Happy is the man that turneth unto Him, and drinketh his fill, and exclaimeth: 'Praise be to Thee, O Revealer of the signs of God!' By the righteousness of the Almighty! Every hidden thing hath been manifested through the power of truth. All the favours of God have been sent down, as a token of His grace. The waters of everlasting life have, in their fullness, been proffered unto men. Every single cup hath been borne round by the hand of the Well-Beloved. Draw near, and tarry not, though it be for one short moment.[1]

Every day, for twelve consecutive days, a steady stream of people came from the city – friends, admirers and well-wishers. Each day Bahá'u'lláh summoned to Him a number of His companions and then dismissed them in the evening. Only those who had no family ties in Baghdád were allowed to remain overnight. Food was sent each day from Bahá'u-'lláh's home in Baghdád and from another Bábí home in the city. The warm winds of spring blew day and night, and Bahá'u'lláh's companions sat on the tent-ropes as His tent was blown night and day, this way and that. Nabíl tells us;

Every day ere the hour of dawn, the gardeners would pick the roses which lined the four avenues of the garden, and would pile them in the centre of the floor of His blessed tent. So great would be the heap that when His companions gathered to drink their morning tea in His presence, they would be unable to see each other across it. All these roses Bahá'u'lláh would, with His own hands, entrust to those whom He dismissed from His presence every morning to be delivered, on His behalf, to His Arab and Persian friends in the city.[2]

In the late evenings the stream of visitors subsided and some of Bahá'u'lláh's companions slept while others watched beside His tent. One night, Nabíl relates:

> . . . the ninth night of the waxing moon, I happened to be one of those who watched beside His blessed tent. As the hour of midnight approached, I saw Him issue from His tent, pass by the places where some of His companions were sleeping, and begin to pace up and down the moonlit, flower-bordered avenues of the garden. So loud was the singing of the nightingales on every side that only those who were near Him could hear distinctly His voice. He continued to walk until, pausing in the midst of one of these avenues, He observed: 'Consider these nightingales. So great is their love for these roses, that sleepless from dusk till dawn, they warble their melodies and commune with burning passion with the object of their adoration. How then can those who claim to be afire with the rose-like beauty of the Beloved choose to sleep?' For three successive nights I watched and circled round His blessed tent. Every time I passed by the couch whereon He lay, I would find Him wakeful, and every day, from morn till eventide, I would see Him ceaselessly engaged in conversing with the stream of visitors who kept flowing in from Baghdád. Not once could I discover in the words He spoke any trace of dissimulation.[3]

The Governor, Námiq Páshá, crossed to the garden one day. He had come, he said, to offer to provide Bahá'u'lláh whatever He might ask for the journey ahead. He asked, also, to be forgiven for what had occurred. Bahá'u'lláh asked nothing of the Governor. He and His companions had, He assured Námiq Páshá, all that was needed for the journey. The Governor then insisted on rendering Him some service.

'Be considerate to My friends', Bahá'u'lláh asked, 'and treat them kindly.'[4]

Námiq Páshá assured Bahá'u'lláh that he would do this. He then wrote a letter and addressed it to the Ottoman officials all along the route from Baghdád to Constantinople, instructing them to provide Bahá'u'lláh and His companions with all necessities. He gave this letter to the official who was assigned to accompany the travellers on their journey to Constantinople.

On the ninth day in the Garden of Riḍván, Bahá'u'lláh's family, their packing almost complete, joined Him and the twelfth day was set for departure. On the morning of that twelfth day, crowds poured across the river yet again, unwilling to miss the chance of a last glimpse of, or a word from, Bahá'u'lláh. The loading of mules took up much of that day and it was late afternoon, towards sunset, before they were ready to start. Most of Bahá'u'lláh's companions were to walk but the women and children were helped into their seats in the jolting howdahs. A red roan stallion, the finest that His companions had been able to obtain, was brought for Bahá'u'lláh. All through the years in Baghdád Bahá'u'lláh had ridden only on a donkey. Now, wearing a tall táj, riding this fine horse and showing a complete mastery of horsemanship, He bade a loving farewell to all who had come to see Him leave. The call to afternoon prayer once again echoed through the flowery avenues, this time as Bahá'u'lláh left that lovely garden.

'Numerous were the heads,' wrote Nabíl, 'which, on every side, bowed to the dust at the feet of His horse, and kissed its hoofs, and countless were those who pressed forward to embrace His stirrups.'[5]

There were cries of distress and of uncontrollable grief. Some even cast themselves on the ground before His horse's hooves. Comforting and consoling others to the last, Bahá'u'lláh left Baghdád. His appearance was kingly and His departure from the city to which he had come as an exile, majestic.

CHAPTER 14

A TRIUMPHAL PROGRESS

WITH all due ceremony Bahá'u'lláh, His family and companions left Baghdád and travelled just three miles north to Firayját. There they stayed for a week while Mírzá Músá wound up all their affairs in Baghdád and organized the final packing and loading of their belongings. At Firayját Bahá'u'lláh stayed in a mansion set in a beautiful garden and, daily, people streamed out from Baghdád to see Him, unwilling to be parted from His presence.

Once Mírzá Músá joined them, the caravan set out in earnest for Constantinople, following the ancient route to the east of the Tigris along which the armies of many empires have marched and fought. There were fifty mules and seven pairs of howdahs in the caravan, each pair of howdahs surmounted by four parasols. The official escort consisted of a mounted Ottoman guard of ten soldiers with their officers. A list prepared for the authorities before their departure gives the names of fifty-four people who were to accompany Bahá'u'lláh to Constantinople. One child died during the journey and at least two people joined the caravan on the way. Siyyid Muḥammad had appealed to 'Abdu'l-Bahá to be included in the party of exiles and Bahá'u'lláh had consented to this, although He had asked Siyyid Muḥammad to remain in Baghdád. Also travelling were two hot-headed individuals, Ḥájí Mírzá Aḥmad from Káshán and Mullá Muḥammad Ja'far from Naráq. Bahá'u'lláh considered it wiser to take them along with Him rather than leave them in Baghdád where they might cause problems for themselves and for the other believers.

Progress was necessarily slow, for a caravan such as this could cover only twenty-five to thirty miles in a day. At every halt the wearisome tasks of unloading and of seeking food and shelter had to be undertaken, every night there were hungry and tired horses and mules to be fed and watered.

Although their Ottoman escort carried the Governor's letter commanding officials in towns and villages through which they passed to supply them with provisions, Bahá'u'lláh would not permit this to happen. He and His party paid for everything they could obtain along the way. Often enough there was little available for either man or beast for the country through which they passed was experiencing famine conditions. The weather was already hot and daily getting hotter on the flat desert land. The caravan often travelled by night to avoid the worst heat of the daytime. Journeying in this fashion was exhausting and as soon as a caravanserai was reached most of the party would fall asleep from sheer weariness.

Almost every time the caravan reached a town, as a result of the written orders of Námiq Páshá, a delegation of Ottoman officials would meet them and on their departure a similar escort would travel with them for some distance beyond the town. At Saláhíyyih, where the local officials and notables held a festival in honour of Bahá'u'lláh and His party, they were able to stay two nights and all were able to rest as guards were also provided to protect them from the danger of highway robbers. On the third night they had to move on even though a gale of hurricane force was blowing and there was neither a moon nor stars to light their way.

From the level plain of 'Iráq they moved slowly into southern Kurdistán. To their right, the east and north, the mountains rose, first the foothills, then the rugged ranges of Kurdistán and beyond those, the high peaks, the rocky ramparts of western Persia. At Karkúk, the largest town in southern Kurdistán, they were able to stop and rest for two days in a pleasant orchard. Beyond Irbíl, on the edge of Kurdistán once again, the prominent men of the town came to greet them and showed a singular respect and reverence towards Bahá'u'lláh.

Over the flat plain of what was once ancient Assyria they wound their slow way to the turbulent waters of the Greater Záb. Here, where once the armies of Assyria, Persia and Rome all forded the river, Bahá'u'lláh and His party crossed the swift and dangerous currents in small boats. Two of their mules were swept clean away and drowned. After resting on the western bank of the river the travellers continued through strong winds to Mosul, close to the site of once-proud Nineveh.

At Mosul Mírzá Yaḥyá joined the caravan in disguise. Five stages of the journey later, at Diyárbakr, he gathered enough courage to reveal his identity to some of the party. In Baghdád, Bahá'u'lláh had told him: 'If you wish to come I will inform Námiq Páshá accordingly; but come in the open.'[1] Mírzá Yaḥyá had been too terrified to do this. First of all he hid in a garden near Baghdád. Then he decided he must leave but not with Bahá'u'lláh's party. Fearful that the entire party would be seized by the Persian authorities while they travelled near the Persian border, he had fled Baghdád in panic during the early days of preparation for the journey.

At Mosul, the city's notables flocked, group after group, to greet and welcome Bahá'u'lláh. The travellers were able to stay three days in that town. They rested and visited the public baths. At Zákhú, three days journey further north, the Qá'im-Maqám, alerted to their approach, sent men to help them bring the clumsy howdahs through rocky defiles that led to the town. He and the notables of the town waited by the roadside in order to pay their respects to Bahá'u'lláh and invited Him to a feast held in His honour. Through Jazírih to Nisíbín they continued towards Márdín where government cavalry bearing flags and beating drums led them along the main street. Nabíl writes of that day:

> As we passed that morning through the town of Márdín, we were preceded by a mounted escort of government soldiers, carrying their banners, and beating their drums in welcome. The mutiṣarrif, together with officials and notables, accompanied us, while men, women and children, crowding the house-tops and filling the streets, awaited our arrival. With dignity and pomp we traversed that town, and resumed our journey, the mutiṣarrif and those with him escorting us for a considerable distance.[2]

This marked reverence towards Bahá'u'lláh and His party is particularly striking as few Persians travelled that way. A traveller visiting Jazírih in the early years of this present century, noted, 'a curious fact that anywhere along the Tigris above Baghdád no Persians exist – nor ever come – and are greater strangers in this out of the way corner than a Greek.[3]

Nabíl reported that:

> According to the unanimous testimony of those we met in the course of that journey, never before had they witnessed along this route, over which governors and mushírs continually passed back and forth between Constantinople and Baghdád, any one travel in such state, dispense such hospitality to all, and accord to each so great a share of his bounty.[4]

Near Ma'dan-i-Mis, Bahá'u'lláh's life was in sudden, terrible danger. The man who was leading the mule which carried Bahá'u'lláh's howdah lost his hold on the reins. The mule lost its footing and started to slide towards the edge of a precipice. The rest of the party watched, appalled but helpless. Somehow, unbelievably it seemed to those onlookers, the animal managed to regain its balance and slowly come to a stop.

Further on, at Khárpút, the officials and notables were, once again, waiting to greet the travellers outside the town. The Governor sent generous gifts of food and fodder. These were most welcome as all were hungry and the pack animals had become lean and could walk only with difficulty. The entire party stayed at Khárpút for a week as Mírzá Muḥammad-ʻAlí, a younger son of Bahá'u'lláh, fell ill there. When he had recovered sufficiently, on they went across the upper Euphrates and through the cool uplands of Anatolia. By the time they reached Amásíyá they had exhausted most of their resources and were obliged to sell some of their horses. They continued through wooded mountains and thick forests across the narrow coastal plain to the shores of the Black Sea. At Sámsún, the Chief Inspector of the province, together with several páshás, waited on Bahá'u'lláh, showing Him great respect. At the port of Sámsún they waited a week for the arrival of an Ottoman steamer which would take them to Constantinople. The steamer carried them westward along the southern coast of the Black Sea and down the Bosporus, the narrow twenty-mile strait that divides the Black Sea from the Sea of Marmara, a voyage of nearly four hundred miles.

CHAPTER 15

HURRIED FROM LAND TO LAND

CONSTANTINOPLE, now called Istanbul, once the capital of the Byzantine Empire, was, when Bahá'u'lláh reached it, the capital of the sprawling Ottoman Empire. It was also the seat of the Caliph, recognized by Sunní Muslims as the rightful successor of the Prophet Muḥammad.

The city, situated at the southern end of the Bosporus, straddles the strait, linking Europe to Asia. Stamboul, the old, walled city, stands on a hilly peninsula bounded on the south by the Sea of Marmara, on the east by the Bosporus and on the north-east by the Golden Horn, a deep, drowned valley. Within the old city are seven flat-topped, steep-sided hills adorned with the soaring minarets and domes of many mosques. To the landward side remnants of the massive walls of the Byzantine city, breached by the Ottoman Turks in 1452, still stand. Near the shore are the long walls and fantastic towers of the Seraglio which was, in 1863, the Sulṭán's palace and the seat of government of the huge Empire.

Carriages were waiting to convey Bahá'u'lláh and His family from the landing-stage to the house of Shamsí Big, the Ottoman official whose job it was to entertain the guests of his government. The rest of the party were given accommodation elsewhere in the city. There were amongst Bahá'u'lláh's companions people from all classes of society, from the highest to the lowest, learned mullás and noblemen mingled with simple tradesmen. Those who had known the advantages of wealth and rank were now overjoyed simply to be allowed to serve in the humblest ways in Bahá'u'lláh's household. Shamsí Big did his best but his house, though spacious, was not roomy enough for Bahá'u'lláh's family.

On the day after His arrival, the Persian Ambassador to the Ottoman court, Ḥájí Mírzá Ḥusayn Khán, sent a respresentative to call on Bahá'u'lláh, to pay his respects and compliments. The Ambassador was being constantly pressured by his government to stir up hostility towards Bahá'u'lláh and thus obtain for Him a more severe banishment. A number of officials and distinguished citizens of the city called on Bahá'u'lláh to pay their respects. Bahá'u'lláh did not return any of these calls, nor did He, as was the custom, attempt to gain an audience with any of the officials or influential people in the capital nor did He ever complain of or criticize the Ottoman or Persian governments. He went out only to the mosque, to the public bath and to His brother's house, once Mírzá Músá obtained a house for his family.

This was unusual behaviour. Constantinople was crowded with exiled Persian princes and noblemen, all of whom schemed and intrigued, seeking allies and financial support for their various designs and pensions for their daily living expenses. Some of His visitors urged Him to call on the Ottoman foreign minister and request an interview with the Grand Vizier who would then consider a request for the visitor to be received by the Sulṭán. When urged to follow this course of action, Bahá'u'lláh is reported to have replied:

> I have no wish to ask favour from them. I have come here at the Sulṭán's command. Whatsoever additional commands he may issue, I am ready to obey. My work is not of their world; it is of another realm, far removed from their province. Why, therefore, should I seek these people?[1]

In a Tablet revealed soon after His arrival in the city, Bahá'u'lláh expressed disappointment in the officials He met in Constantinople. Their welcome for Him was, He wrote, a mere formality. He found them, He said, without exception, as cold as ice and as lifeless as dead trees. Later, in Adrianople, He wrote of His arrival in Constantinople:

> We found, upon Our arrival in the City, its governors and elders as children gathered about and disporting themselves with clay. We perceived no one sufficiently mature to acquire from Us the truths which God hath taught Us, nor ripe for Our wondrous words of wisdom. Our inner eye wept sore over them, and over their transgressions and their total disregard of the thing for which they were created.[2]

After one month in the cramped conditions of Shamsí Big's overcrowded house, a larger house, three-storied, with its own Turkish bath and a vast garden was provided for the use of the exiles. A tent was pitched in the courtyard for two Christian servants whom the government paid to attend to shopping and other duties. Shamsí Big came himself every morning to enquire if there was any matter that needed his own attention.

As the summer ended, the exiles had to accustom themselves to a very different climate from that of 'Iráq. The great rivers of Russia and Europe that pour into the Black Sea thrust their cold waters southward under the warm waters which swell north from the Mediterranean, bringing in the winter months cold rains and mists and grey, choppy seas, a stark contrast to the brilliant sunlight of 'Iráq.

Outwardly all appeared calm but Ḥájí Mírzá Ḥusayn Khán resented the fact that Bahá'u'lláh had not sought any favours from him nor from the Ottoman court. Under constant pressure from those in Ṭihrán who feared and hated Bahá'u'lláh, he spread word in official circles and through the capital that Bahá'u'lláh was a proud and arrogant individual Whose own actions were the cause of His banishment first to 'Iráq and now to Constantinople. It was as a direct result of the persistent intrigues of this Ambassador that the attitude of the authorities towards Bahá'u'lláh became hostile.

Bahá'u'lláh and His family had been living in the large house for less than three months when an envoy from the Ottoman court came to the house, seeking an interview with Him. Bahá'u'lláh delegated 'Abdu'l-Bahá and Mírzá Músá to receive him. This envoy brought the news that Bahá'u'lláh, His family and companions had been banished by the Sulṭán to Adrianople. They were to proceed there without delay. The envoy announced that he would return in three days to receive a response to the edict.

That same day Bahá'u'lláh revealed a Tablet, addressed to the Grand Vizier, 'Alí Páshá, who, together with Fu'ad Páshá, the Minister of Foreign Affairs, had obtained the Sulṭán's consent to the edict of banishment. The next morning, Shamsí Big personally delivered this Tablet, in a sealed envelope, to 'Alí Páshá.

'I know not what that letter contained,' Shamsí Big later told Mírzá Músá, 'for no sooner had the Grand Vizir perused it than he turned the colour of a corpse, and remarked: "It is as if the King of Kings were issuing his behest to his humblest vassal king and regulating his conduct." So grievous was his condition that I backed out of His presence.'[3]

This Tablet has not survived but it is certain that in it Bahá'u'lláh severely condemned the decision made to banish Him.

'Whatever action', Bahá'u'lláh commented when told of the Grand Vizier's reaction to the Tablet, 'the ministers of the Sulṭán took against Us, after having become acquainted with its contents, cannot be regarded as unjustifiable. The acts they committed before its perusal, however, can have no justification.'[4]

Áqá Riḍá, a Bábí from Shíráz, an eye-witness of those days in Constantinople, later in his life recalled that

Bahá'u'lláh encouraged all those with Him to stand firm and to refuse to accept this humiliating banishment. They had done nothing wrong, Bahá'u'lláh assured them. They had come to Constantinople at the invitation of the government and now, without any cause or reason, they were being banished, precipitately, to a remote corner of the Ottoman Empire. There could be no better time for them all to offer up their lives.

'Truly,' Áqá Riḍá recalled, 'at that time, all of us, with the utmost joy, fidelity, unity and detachment, were eager to attain to that high station; and God is my witness that we were blissfully expecting martyrdom.'[5]

However, at this juncture Mírzá Yaḥyá, Siyyid Muḥammad and Ḥájí Mízrá Aḥmad-i-Ká<u>sh</u>ání pleaded that their wives and children would suffer greatly without them. When this line of argument failed, they began to scheme together as to how they might save their own lives. When Bahá'u'lláh saw this, He reluctantly agreed to accept the order of banishment.

'They called us here, as their guests,' He said, as Áqá Riḍá recalled, 'and innocent as we are, they turned on us with vengeance. If we, few as we are, had stood our ground to fall martyrs in the midmost heart of the world, the effect of that martyrdom would have been felt in all the worlds of God. And possibly nothing would have happened to us.'[6]

Even while hurried preparations were made for their imminent departure, the notables of the city still came to call on Bahá'u'lláh. A number of Bábís reached the city also, with the one aim of gaining Bahá'u'lláh's presence. Bahá'u'lláh advised them to leave at once for He did not want, for their own safety and that of the other believers, more Bábís to gather in the Ottoman capital.

His banishment, He knew, had been brought about by the combined pressure of the Persian and Ottoman governments. On the eve of His departure, in a last interview with the envoy of the Persian Ambassador, He sent these words to Ḥájí Mírzá Ḥusayn K͟hán:

> What did it profit thee, and such as are like thee, to slay, year after year, so many of the oppressed, and to inflict upon them manifold afflictions, when they have increased a hundred-fold, and ye find yourselves in complete bewilderment, knowing not how to relieve your minds of this oppressive thought . . . His Cause transcends any and every plan ye devise. Know this much: Were all the governments on earth to unite and take My life and the lives of all who bear this Name, this Divine Fire would never be quenched. His Cause will rather encompass all the kings of the earth, nay all that hath been created from water and clay . . . Whatever may yet befall Us, great shall be our gain, and manifest the loss wherewith they shall be afflicted.[7]

The night before His departure, Bahá'u'lláh directed Nabíl and one other believer to travel to Persia in order to spread the news of His declaration among the believers, to deepen them in the teachings and to help them recognize His station. He left in Constantinople just one of His companions whose task would be to act as a channel of communication between Adrianople and the believers in Persia. The others He urged to leave the city and to teach the Faith in their homeland. The party departing for Adrianople consisted of His family and twelve of His companions, amongst them Siyyid Muḥammad.

Carriages, wagons, pack-animals and ox-carts were provided by the government but it was midwinter in a season of exceptionally severe weather, the coldest for forty years. The prevailing wind in Constantinople is from the north-east but in winter an icy north-west wind from the Balkans brings a freezing blast, the Karayel or Black Veil, which is capable of freezing the Golden Horn and even the Bosporus.

'A cold of such intensity', Nabíl relates, 'prevailed that year, that nonagenarians could not recall its like.'[8]

None of the party had adequate clothing for the journey and it was snowing as they left the city. Across a flat, bleak and windy landscape, accompanied by Turkish military officers, they wound their way on a twelve-day journey, sometimes through the bitter-cold nights, often in rain and storm. Ḥusayn-i-Á<u>sh</u><u>ch</u>í, a Bábí who had joined the exiles soon after they left Ba<u>gh</u>dád and who had now become the cook for Bahá'u'lláh's household, saw a number of people frozen to death by the roadside. Bahíyyih <u>Kh</u>ánum, already delicate, suffered greatly from the cold and felt the effects of that particular midwinter journey of exile to the end of her life.

It was, Nabíl wrote: 'A banishment endured with such meekness that the pen sheddeth tears when recounting it and the page is ashamed to bear its description.'[9]

CHAPTER 16

DAYS OF STRESS

EDIRNE, as Adrianople is now called, is a border town of the present-day Turkish republic. It stands in a loop of the river Tunja just above the Tunja's junction with the Maritsa. The Maritsa rises in Bulgaria and meanders through a wide flood plain to the sea. Situated on Europe's most easterly promontory, the climate is a harsh and dry one; bitter winters alternate with scorching summers.

Edirne is an ancient city. Once the main town of the Thracians, it was rebuilt by the Emperor Hadrian in the second century AD and renamed by him Adrianople. In 1362 the Ottoman Turks took Adrianople from the weakening Byzantines and for almost fifty years before they captured Constantinople it was the capital of their expanding empire. When Constantinople became the Ottoman capital, Adrianople remained for centuries an important administrative and commercial centre and the main gateway to the Balkan lands.

It was also for several centuries a favourite haunt of many of the Ottoman rulers. They built there a number of beautiful mosques whose splendid domes and minarets make it appear the most oriental of all Turkish cities. Nearby was a vast marshy area teeming with wildfowl where many of the sulṭáns hunted. Its summer climate, though hot, is more bracing than that of the capital and in previous centuries the entire court had sometimes moved to Adrianople during the summer months to escape the enervating heat.

By the time that Bahá'u'lláh was sent there the city had suffered greatly under a Russian occupation in 1828–9 and was no longer a spot favoured by the sulṭáns. It was still a city with a hundred thousand inhabitants but Bahá'u'lláh wrote of it as the remote prison, 'the place which none entereth except such as have rebelled against the authority of the sovereign'.[1]

This was the furthest north and the farthest from His homeland that Bahá'u'lláh was to travel. The bitter weather persisted. That first winter the exiles spent in Adrianople was the hardest its people had experienced for almost half a century. On their arrival the travellers spent three days and nights crowded into a comfortless caravanserai. Then a small house was found for Bahá'u'lláh in the north-eastern section of the city. He and His family moved there. The rest of the party remained at the caravanserai and meals were brought to them from the house of Bahá'u'lláh. Then a more spacious house in the same quarter was obtained. Some of those at the inn moved into the house that Bahá'u'lláh vacated and a third house was rented close by for Mírzá Músá and Mírzá Yaḥyá and their families.

All three houses were old, poorly constructed and draughty. The exiles, inadequately clothed and unaccustomed to the harsh winter climate of this corner of Europe, suffered greatly. A stove was kept alight in Bahá'u'lláh's room but in spite of this a jug of water froze there one night. The public baths had to remain closed for several days that winter and the springs of the city froze hard. There were frequent snowfalls well into spring.

Money also was in short supply and food was of the plainest. However, Áqá Ḥusayn-i-As͟hc͟hí, now the cook for Bahá'u'lláh's household, managed to obtain two cows and a goat and thus was able to supply the household with milk and yoghurt. Despite all the hardships of that year, the companions of Bahá'u'lláh were happy simply to be near Him and to serve Him. They lived close to Him, were often in His presence and they asked for nothing more.

The Persian and Ottoman governments had combined, so they imagined, to humiliate Bahá'u'lláh. In Constantinople He had been a guest of the Governor; here He was officially a prisoner, although no formal charges had been brought against Him. He visited the mosques but otherwise He led a retired life. He walked only in the garden of His house or in a vineyard rented by Mírzá Muḥammad-Qulí.

However, as outwardly His situation became bleaker, He revealed a flood of majestic, awe-inspiring Tablets. As the two absolute rulers of the two empires strove to conceal Him from men, Bahá'u'lláh clearly proclaimed His mission in Tablets directed to the kings and rulers of the world, both secular and ecclesiastic, and, through them, to the peoples of the entire planet.

In Adrianople, although Bahá'u'lláh did not move about the city as freely as He had done in Baghdád, His presence was soon felt by the leading men of the city and by the ordinary citizens. As before, He gave food to the needy and organized a soup kitchen. Mírzá Yaḥyá, though inwardly consumed with jealousy, remained, for the moment, outwardly subdued. But so overwhelming was the jealousy and hatred he now nursed against his brother that about a year after their arrival in Adrianople he began to scheme as to how he might bring about Bahá'u'lláh's death.

After about ten months in that second house, a much more spacious house, a mansion, close to the centre of the city was found, the house of Amru'lláh, which means 'The House of God's Command'. Its inner quarter alone contained thirty rooms, amongst them a set of splendid reception rooms. The house had its own Turkish bath, a supply of running water in the kitchen and a place for the storage of water. Two other houses were rented nearby for Mírzá Músá and Mírzá Yaḥyá and their families. All the meals were prepared in the house of Amru'lláh and conveyed daily to the other houses.

Bahá'u'lláh now encouraged those who were not occupied in serving their companions to support themselves financially by engaging in a trade or similar activity. Several opened shops, one began to weave silk, another worked as a tailor. In the evenings the companions gathered at the house of Amru'lláh, in the daytime they went about their trades, all except for Siyyid Muḥammad and Ḥájí Mírzá Aḥmad, the hot-tempered Bábí from Káshán.

These two did not choose to follow Bahá'u'lláh's counsel to work. Rather, during the second year of Bahá'u'lláh's residence in the House of Amru'lláh they began to stir up dissension in the community. It was done very secretly but the other Bábís became aware of the intrigue and met frequently to say prayers for the whole community. Siyyid Muḥammad's jealousy of Bahá'u'lláh had not abated. It became daily more intense in the face of Bahá'u'lláh's obvious leadership of the Bábí community and His rising prestige in the city.

Mírzá Yaḥyá too was watching for his chance to harm Bahá'u'lláh. Poison was the obvious first choice, for Mírzá Músá knew a great deal about plants, those that could heal and those that could kill. Under the pretence of wishing to study the healing arts, Mírzá Yaḥyá learnt all that he could from his unsuspecting half-brother. His first attempt at causing damage was to poison the well from which Bahá'u'lláh and His family took their water. As a result, they began to experience inexplicable symptoms of sickness.

Then he began to invite Bahá'u'lláh to his house, something he had never done before. There, one day, he smeared a teacup with a poison he had concocted and served tea in it to Bahá'u'lláh. Bahá'u'lláh fell gravely ill at once with a high fever and severe pains. A Bulgarian doctor, a certain Dr Shíshmán, was called to treat Him. Dr Shíshmán, horrified at Bahá'u'lláh's condition, deemed His case hopeless and recovery impossible. He fell at Bahá'u'lláh's feet and then left without even prescribing a remedy. A few days later Dr Shíshmán himself fell gravely ill. Mírzá Áqá Ján, sent by Bahá'u'lláh to visit the sick physician, reported on a strange conversation. Dr Shíshmán, he said, stated that God had answered his prayer and that after his death a certain Dr Chúpán, whom he recommended as a reliable physician, should be summoned in his stead. A few days later Dr Shíshmán died. Before his death occurred, Bahá'u'lláh intimated that the doctor had sacrificed his life for Him. Bahá'u'lláh slowly recovered though He remained seriously ill for an entire month.

Then, over a period of three months, Mírzá Yaḥyá worked his way into what he hoped would be the confidence of Bahá'u'lláh's barber and hinted, obliquely, that he should, when an opportune moment arose, murder Bahá'u'lláh while He was attending the public bath. So appalled at such a notion was this barber, Ustád Muḥammad-'Alíy-i-Salmání, that he was unable to heed 'Abdu'l-Bahá's advice and then even Bahá'u'lláh's request to keep this matter to himself. He soon betrayed his secret and thus plunged the entire community into consternation.

Bahá'u'lláh now ordered Mírzá Áqá Ján to carry to Mírzá Yaḥyá a newly-revealed Tablet, the Súriy-i-Amr, in which Bahá'u'lláh's claim to be the One Whose coming the Báb had foretold is clearly and emphatically stated. Mírzá Áqá Ján was, He instructed, to read the Tablet aloud to Mírzá Yaḥyá and demand an immediate and unequivocal reply. On hearing this Tablet, Mírzá Yaḥyá requested a day in which to meditate on a reply. This request was granted but the only reply was a counter-claim by Mírzá Yaḥyá, in which he specified the exact date and time he had himself received a revelation from God.

Once again, as in the early days in Baghdád, Bahá'u'lláh chose to provide complete freedom for the Bábís to choose between Him and His half-brother. All the possessions in

His home, He told Mírzá Músá, must be divided and half sent to Mírzá Yaḥyá. Certain precious objects connected with the Báb, His seals, rings and manuscripts, these too must be given to Mírzá Yaḥyá. Mírzá Músá was to ensure that Mírzá Yaḥyá received every part of the government allowance allotted to him. One of the exiles must attend to Mírzá Yaḥyá's shopping and, finally, anything that arrived from Persia must be delivered immediately to him. The other exiles too must also receive their allowance and not one of them was to visit Bahá'u'lláh until He gave permission again.

Mírzá Músá faithfully carried out these instructions while Bahá'u'lláh withdrew, with His immediate family, to another house, the house of Riḍá Big. On only one day, soon after He moved to the house of Riḍá Big, did Bahá'u'lláh allow His grieving companions to visit Him. He advised them to trust in God, to be patient and to avoid conflict with anyone. For two months, Bahá'u'lláh remained in seclusion.

'Those days', one of the followers of Bahá'u'lláh wrote, 'were marked by tumult and confusion. We were sore-perplexed, and greatly feared lest we be permanently deprived of the bounty of His presence.'[2]

Siyyid Muḥammad and Mírzá Yaḥyá plunged ahead with their schemes, unrestrained and unhindered. They wrote slanderous letters to the authorities in Persia, blackening Bahá'u'lláh's name. Siyyid Muḥammad travelled to Constantinople and there begged from the Persian Ambassador a stipend both for himself and for Mírzá Yaḥyá. Bahá'u'lláh, he claimed, had despatched an agent to Persia to assassinate the Sháh.

Back in Adrianople, Mírzá Yaḥyá sent one of his wives to the government offices. He had been cheated of his rights, he stated. His children were about to starve. These rumours spread as far as Constantinople and did considerable damage amongst the officials and notables who had been so deeply impressed by Bahá'u'lláh's behaviour when He had lived in the city. Malicious letters were sent also to Khurshíd Páshá, the newly-appointed Governor of Adrianople, and to his deputy, 'Azíz Páshá.

Khurshíd Páshá, appointed to the governorship in March of 1866, had quickly become aware of Bahá'u'lláh's rare qualities. Puzzled by these slanderous letters, he brought them to Bahá'u'lláh. When Bahá'u'lláh read them He knew that He could no longer remain in seclusion.

'We secluded ourselves', He is reported to have said, 'that perchance the fire of hostility might be quenched, and such disgraceful acts be averted, but they have resorted to measures more extreme than before.'[3]

Bahá'u'lláh emerged from His self-imposed isolation and once more took up the task of guiding the other Bábís. He sent two loyal followers to Constantinople so that they might attempt to repair some of the damage done there by Siyyid Muḥammad. But from this time on, because of the harm already done by Siyyid Muḥammad's slanderous accusations, He refused to draw any of the Ottoman government's allowance to which He and His family were entitled. He was thus obliged to sell some of His belongings in order to provide for His family.

Bahá'u'lláh dissociated Himself completely from His half-brother and a separation came about between Bahá'u'lláh and His loyal followers and the few Bábís who listened to the claims made by Siyyid Muḥammad and Mírzá Yaḥyá. From this time on, the followers of Mírzá Yaḥyá were sometimes called Azalís, followers of Azal, from the title Ṣubḥ-i-Azal, Morning of Eternity, earlier given to Mírzá Yaḥyá, by the Báb. After this, Bahá'u'lláh often addressed them as 'the people of the Bayán'.

Mírzá Yaḥyá continued as before to live in virtual seclusion, unwilling to abandon his hopes of leadership. Bahá'u'lláh spent about one year in the house of Riḍá Big, then three months once again in the House of Amru'lláh.

Then, as the owner of the house needed it back, another large house, the House of 'Izzat Áqá, in a more distant quarter of the city, was rented.

Life for the exiles continued thus until September of 1867 when a certain Mír Muḥammad, a Bábí of Shíráz, resenting both Mírzá Yaḥyá's claims and his refusal to meet openly with the other Bábís, persuaded him to agree to meet with Bahá'u'lláh face to face in a public forum – a tradition well-respected in Islám – and debate the issue of leadership so that, as he stated, all might be able to discriminate between truth and falsity. Mírzá Yaḥyá agreed to this suggestion only because he never imagined that Bahá'u'lláh would accept this challenge. He named the mosque of Sulṭán Salím as the meeting-place.

As soon as this invitation reached Bahá'u'lláh, He accepted it. On the appointed day, accompanied only by Mír Muḥammad, He set out, on foot, in the noonday heat, for the appointed meeting-place, some distance across the city. Word of the proposed meeting had spread through the city, through the Muslim, Jewish and Christian communities. A large crowd gathered outside Bahá'u'lláh's house and along the way to the mosque. As He walked through the streets, He recited, in stirring tones and to the amazement of the onlookers, these and other challenging verses:

> O Muḥammad! He Who is the Spirit hath, verily, issued from His habitation, and with Him have come forth the souls of God's chosen ones and the realities of His Messengers. Behold, then, the dwellers of the realms on high above Mine head, and all the testimonies of the Prophets in My grasp. Say: Were all the divines, all the wise men, all the kings and rulers on earth to gather together, I, in very truth, would confront them, and would proclaim the verses of God, the Sovereign, the Almighty, the All-Wise. I am He Who feareth no one, though all who are in heaven and all who are on earth rise up against me.[4]

Arriving at the mosque, Bahá'u'lláh sent Mír Muḥammad to call Mírzá Yaḥyá to come and face his Lord. Mírzá Yaḥyá and Siyyid Muḥammad did not appear though Bahá'u'lláh waited in the mosque until sunset. Mír Muḥammad brought from Mírzá Yaḥyá a message that, due to unforeseen circumstances, he was obliged to postpone the interview for a day or two. On returning to His house, Bahá'u'lláh revealed a Tablet relating all that had occurred, fixed another date and time for the interview and arranged for this Tablet to be delivered to Mírzá Yaḥyá. He stipulated, however, that this Tablet should not be delivered until Mírzá Yaḥyá would admit, in writing, that avoidance of this interview amounted to an admission that his claims were false. The Tablet was never delivered for Mírzá Yaḥyá was not willing to make such a pledge.

This internal crisis, which appeared to outsiders as a schism within the Bábí community, brought untold sorrow to Bahá'u'lláh. It was, as Shoghi Effendi describes it, 'the heaviest blow' of His lifetime. It 'visibly aged Him' and caused Him 'incalculable sorrow'.[5] It was the most severe ordeal that the Bábí community had yet experienced and it was to linger on and leave its mark for half a century. It confused and disturbed new-found friends and supporters. It provided just the chance for which the external enemies of the new Faith were waiting to launch fresh assaults on the exiles and their fellow-believers in 'Iráq and Persia.

CHAPTER 17

LAND OF MYSTERY

THROUGHOUT this period of stress, Bahá'u'lláh experienced great anguish.

'He who for months and years I reared with the hand of loving-kindness', He wrote, 'hath arisen to take My life.'[1] Addressing Mírzá Yaḥyá He sadly wrote: 'No spot is left on My body that hath not been touched by the spears of thy machinations'[2] and, reflecting on this most agonizing time of stress and contention, He lamented:

> The cruelties inflicted by My oppressors have bowed Me down, and turned My hair white. Shouldst thou present thyself before My throne, thou wouldst fail to recognize the Ancient Beauty, for the freshness of His countenance is altered, and its brightness hath faded, by reason of the oppression of the infidels.[3]

Despite the searing agony of those days, though He had not fully recovered from the effects of the poison administered by Mírzá Yaḥyá and though He was aware that another banishment more harsh than any yet experienced was imminent, Bahá'u'lláh, both during and after that severe ordeal, revealed a virtual torrent of Tablets proclaiming His mission.

The severity of the crisis through which the new Faith passed was matched by an unprecedented outpouring of inspired guidance. Almost immediately after Bahá'u'lláh dissociated Himself from His half-brother, some of the most powerful and significant of all His writings were revealed.

'A number of secretaries', Nabíl recorded, 'were busy day and night and yet they were unable to cope with the task.

Among them was Mírzá Báqir-i-Shírází . . . He alone transcribed no less than two thousand verses every day. He laboured during six or seven months. Every month the equivalent of several volumes would be transcribed by him and sent to Persia.'[4]

'So great is the grace', Bahá'u'lláh Himself wrote, 'vouchsafed in this day that in a single day and night, were an amanuensis capable of accomplishing it to be found, the equivalent of the Persian Bayán would be sent down from the heaven of Divine holiness.'[5]

Bahá'u'lláh had gradually revealed His mission, at first to a handful of the Bábí community in Baghdád in the Riḍván garden, then to other members of the Bábí community. In Constantinople, with the Tablet addressed to Sulṭán 'Abdu'l-'Azíz He had begun to announce His mission to the rest of the world. In Adrianople, while the most grievous crisis caused by Mírzá Yaḥyá and Siyyid Muḥammad still rocked the community, He continued revealing letters to the world's rulers. The announcement of His mission reached a majestic climax with the Tablet to the Kings, a stirring Tablet in which He, an exile, warned and admonished the crowned rulers of that period.

> Lay not aside the fear of God, O kings of the earth, and beware that ye transgress not the bounds which the Almighty hath fixed . . . Compose your differences, and reduce your armaments, that the burden of your expenditures may be lightened . . . Rest not on your power, your armies, and your treasures . . . Know ye that the poor are the trust of God in your midst. Watch that ye betray not His trust, that ye deal not unjustly with them . . . Ye will most certainly be called upon to answer for His trust on the day when the Balance of Justice shall be set . . .[6]

During the last months that He spent in the House of 'Izzat, Bahá'u'lláh revealed a long Tablet for the Sháh, the longest of any He wrote to all the rulers, but did not send it.

It waited, He said, for the person who would be worthy to deliver it. He also wrote a powerful Tablet to the French ruler, Napoleon III, and sent it to him. He revealed the moving Tablet of the Branch in which He alludes to the unique station He was to bestow upon 'Abdu'l-Bahá. The eloquent and soul-stirring prayers for fasting also date from this time.

Several other significant events took place during this period. Bahá'u'lláh instructed the friends in Ṭihrán to move the precious remains of the Báb and Anís from the shrine of the Imám-Zádih to a safer place. He sent Nabíl to Shíráz and to Baghdád where he carried out, at the house of the Báb and the house of Bahá'u'lláh, the rites of pilgrimage prescribed by Bahá'u'lláh for future pilgrims. The first pilgrims to Adrianople began to arrive, believers who had travelled all the way from Persia and 'Iráq in order to attain to the presence of Bahá'u'lláh.

As a direct result of the dissension and division caused by Mírzá Yaḥyá, several outstanding disciples of Bahá'u'lláh arose to defend the Faith in writing, refuting the arguments put forward by 'the people of the Bayán', as Mírzá Yaḥyá and his followers were now known, in contrast to 'the people of Bahá', the followers of Bahá'u'lláh. The greeting 'Alláh-u-Abhá', meaning 'God is most Glorious', was adopted simultaneously by the believers in both Persia and Adrianople.

Those who wished to destroy the new Faith took advantage of the internal crisis in Adrianople to strike at the Bábís. In Baghdád a devoted follower of Bahá'u'lláh was brutally disembowelled. Seventy of the believers of Baghdád and Káẓimayn, men, women and children, were rounded up and ignominiously banished to Mosul. In Persia, savage persecution broke out in Ádharbáyján, in Zanján, Níshápúr and in Ṭihrán. But at the same time, the new Faith spread to the Caucasus, to Egypt and to Syria.

In Constantinople the authorities, alarmed at the reports

of pilgrims arriving in Adrianople, tried but failed to stem the flow. Believers continued to arrive. The Governor of Adrianople, his deputy and other notables of the city continued to demonstrate a remarkable respect and admiration for Bahá'u'lláh. During the period of Ramaḍán, the Governor invited Bahá'u'lláh to a splendid reception and dinner. There the leading men of the city, men of wealth and culture, sat as humble disciples in Bahá'u'lláh's presence, marvelling at His words.

In Constantinople the authorities grew increasingly alarmed. Fu'ad Pásh͟há, on a tour of inspection, sent in an exaggerated account of the veneration paid to Bahá'u'lláh. Infuriated by K͟hursh͟híd Pásh͟há's attitude towards the Exile in his charge, deeply conscious of the unstable conditions existing in their empire and alarmed by the exaggerated claims of some over-zealous Bahá'ís in Constantinople itself, the Ottoman ministers became thoroughly frightened. Siyyid Muḥammad now sent more letters to the capital, accusing Bahá'u'lláh of plotting with Bulgarian leaders and with certain European powers to capture Constantinople.

This was too much; the authorities took action. In April of 1868 the Bahá'ís of Adrianople were rounded up and interrogated. These interrogations lasted for several weeks. Each time the companions were counted one by one and their names recorded. Each time they did not know if they would be able to return to their homes. Rumours spread that they were to be banished, scattered or put to death.

In Constantinople the authorities arrested Bahá'u'lláh's emissaries and when three more arrived, charged by Bahá'u'lláh with the task of selling some valuable Arab horses which had been given to Him, they were thrown into prison immediately they set foot in the city. Since Bahá'u'lláh was no longer drawing a government allowance, these horses were to be sold to provide money for daily living expenses. Bahá'u'lláh advised some of the Bahá'ís to leave

Adrianople at once. Incoming pilgrims received the same advice.

On 26 July, the Ottoman ministers Alí Pá<u>sh</u>á and Fu'ad Pá<u>sh</u>á obtained the Sulṭán's consent for a further banishment of Bahá'u'lláh. An imperial edict of that date orders the banishment of Bahá'u'lláh to the prison fortress of 'Akká and to life imprisonment within its walls. This order was sent directly to the Governor of Adrianople with instructions for it to be conveyed to Bahá'u'lláh.

The Governor was unwilling to carry out his government's orders. This he told to Bahá'u'lláh, expressing his abhorrence of the order he had received. He moved quietly out of the city, ostensibly to a distant location and left the job to his deputy.

Late one night Bahá'u'lláh instructed three of His followers, two of whom had only recently arrived from Persia, to leave Adrianople at once, that very night, and return to Persia. The very next day the Bahá'ís of the city were rounded up early in the morning and brought to the government headquarters. One by one they were questioned in order to make them admit that they were Bahá'ís. Their goods were seized and sold at auction. The same day, early in the morning, soldiers surrounded the house of Bahá'u-'lláh. No one was able to go in or out. An officer reported to 'Abdu'l-Bahá that Bahá'u'lláh and His family were to proceed to Gallipoli within two days.

CHAPTER 18

TO THE DESOLATE CITY

THE details of the imperial edict were not shared with the exiles. Bahá'u'lláh was simply ordered to leave Adrianople with His family and the twelve companions who had come with Him from Constantinople and to proceed to Gallipoli. No one was given any idea of any further destination.

Bahá'u'lláh replied to the authorities that they could not leave within two days. His household steward owed a large sum of money in the bazaar. This debt could not be paid until His horses were sold in Constantinople and this could not be achieved while His followers were detained in the capital.

That first night the exiles were left without food as soldiers stood guard around the house. Neighbours and others surrounded the house and a considerable commotion arose. No one knew why the Bahá'ís were being treated in this way. They were respected and Bahá'u'lláh was revered. They worked for their living, they were law-abiding, they had been kind and generous to all.

'The people surrounded the house,' Bahá'u'lláh was soon to write, 'and Muslims and Christians wept over Us . . . We perceived that the weeping of the people of the Son (Christians) exceeded the weeping of others – a sign for such as ponder.'[1]

Two of Bahá'u'lláh's companions later recounted that the foreign consuls of several European powers called to ask if they might be of assistance in helping to reverse the edict. Bahá'u'lláh politely declined these offers of assistance.

The distress amongst the exiles was intense. One man,

knowing that his name was not on the list of those ordered to accompany Bahá'u'lláh, slit his own throat and only submitted to medical treatment when Bahá'u'lláh Himself promised that he should join the exiles as soon as he recovered. Two of the exiles were forced to divorce their wives, since their relatives would not allow them to travel with their husbands. None of the exiles wished to stay behind; all were determined to accompany Bahá'u'lláh wherever He might be sent. Several pilgrims, arriving in Adrianople, went straight on to Gallipoli without even catching a glimpse of Bahá'u'lláh.

Ḥusayn-i-Á<u>sh</u><u>ch</u>í later recalled that Bahá'u'lláh insisted that all the believers must accompany Him and that the Ottoman authorities responded with a cable agreeing to this. Bahá'u'lláh refused to accept the money allotted to meet His own travelling expenses and returned it to the Governor. His loyal followers still held in Constantinople were released and sent directly to Gallipoli: money in part payment for the horses was sent to Adrianople.

In early August luggage was loaded into carts and several of the believers set off with them. At the same time Mírzá Yaḥyá and Siyyid Muḥammad left for Gallipoli. A week later, arrangements for Bahá'u'lláh's own departure were complete.

On 12 August 1868 several more carts were loaded with the rest of the luggage and around noon the members of Bahá'u'lláh's own family climbed into them. A crowd had gathered to say goodbye to the exiles. When Baha'u'lláh took His leave the people came, one by one, to bid Him a sorrowful farewell. Escorted by a Turkish captain, Ḥasan Effendi, and other soldiers, the exiles left the city that had been their home for five years.

The journey to Gallipoli took four full days. Many of the believers walked. If any strayed from the group or fell asleep and were thus left behind, Bahá'u'lláh would refuse to proceed until horsemen were despatched to search for and find them. Whenever any of the believers lamented their possible separation from Him, Ḥusayn-i-Ás͟hc͟hí recalled, tears would flow down His cheeks.

During the journey Bahá'u'lláh wrote the Súriy-i-Ra'ís, a powerful Tablet addressed to 'Alí Pás͟há, the Ottoman Grand Vizier:

> The day is approaching when the Land of Mystery (Adrianople), and what is beside it shall be changed, and shall pass out of the hands of the king, and commotions shall appear, and the voice of lamentation shall be raised, and the evidences of mischief shall be revealed on all sides, and confusion shall spread by reason of that which hath befallen these captives at the hands of the hosts of oppression.[2]

On arrival in Adrianople the exiles met up with their companions sent there from Constantinople but there was still no word of their final destination. Rumours multiplied. They would be scattered, they would be exterminated, they would, the greatest misery of all, be separated from Bahá'u'lláh. One night when Ḥasan Effendi came to take his leave and return to Adrianople, Bahá'u'lláh asked him to give a message to the Sulṭán.

'Tell the king', He said, 'that this territory will pass out of his hands, and his affairs will be thrown into confusion. Not I speak these words, but God speaketh them.'[3]

These sentences were uttered with such power and authority that it seemed to those who heard them in the room below the very foundations of the house trembled.

For three days all waited in suspense. Then the terms of the original order were made known. Bahá'u'lláh and His two loyal brothers, Mírzá Músá and Mírzá Muḥammad-Qulí, were to be sent to 'Akká; the rest were to proceed to Constantinople. Mírzá Yaḥyá was to be sent to Cyprus. The distress was at once deep and clamorous. At the insistence of

Bahá'u'lláh and with the help of 'Umar Effendi, a major appointed to accompany the exiles, the edict was changed.

New instructions were issued that all, except for four of Bahá'u'lláh's faithful companions, were to proceed to 'Akká. These four were the four Bahá'ís first arrested in Constantinople. They were directed to accompany Mírzá Yaḥyá to exile in Cyprus while several of the Azalís, the followers of Mírzá Yaḥyá, were directed to 'Akká. However, only those named on the list were allowed to travel at government expense. To the amazement of 'Umar Effendi and the other officials, some of those not on the list bought their own tickets. Never before had these officials encountered people who would willingly buy their way to imprisonment in a strange land.

Bahá'u'lláh solemnly warned His companions that 'this journey will be unlike any of the previous journeys'.[4] Whoever did not feel that he could face the unknown perils ahead of them all had better 'depart to whatever place he pleaseth, and be preserved from tests, for hereafter he will find himself unable to leave.'[5] Not one of the exiles chose to follow this advice.

Bahá'u'lláh and His companions embarked on a crowded Austrian Lloyd steamer bound for Alexandria. There they transhipped onto a vessel bound for Haifa via Port Said and Jaffa. They had not been allowed time to buy adequate provisions for the journey and had only a few loaves of bread and a little cheese given to them by friends. Most were worn out and anxious. They became seasick but there was no room to lie down in the boat and there was besides a most terrible stench. By the time they reached Haifa the women in the party were so weak and ill that they had to be carried ashore in chairs.

Here in Haifa the exiles were to part company. Mírzá Yaḥyá and the four Bahá'ís already selected to accompany him were detailed to leave the larger group and travel on a

The Mosque of Sulṭán Salím in Adrianople, visited occasionally by Bahá'u'lláh.

The Sea Wall of 'Akká.

separate boat to Cyprus. As Bahá'u'lláh stepped from the quay into the boat that was to take Him to the landing-stage in Haifa, 'Abdu'l-Ghaffár, doomed to accompany Mírzá Yaḥyá to Cyprus, leapt into the sea, choosing a watery grave rather than separation from Bahá'u'lláh. He was rescued and resuscitated with difficulty. Bahá'u'lláh consoled him and encouraged him to proceed to Cyprus.

In Haifa they had to wait for a few hours on the dockside before embarking in a sailing vessel for the last leg of the journey to 'Akká. It was very, very hot and there was no breeze. There was no shade in the boat, no shelter from the burning sun. It took eight miserable hours to cross the bay to 'Akká. On arrival the women were so prostrated by heat and sickness that once again they had all to be carried ashore in chairs.

CHAPTER 19

THE MOST GREAT PRISON

It was late afternoon on the last day of August in 1868 that Bahá'u'lláh and His companions, seventy in number, reached the prison city. Beneath the gaping mouths of the cannon which guarded the harbour, the exiles entered 'Akká through the sea gate, a narrow doorway in the massive defensive wall of the fortress city. The heavy wooden door, lapped with iron bands, was swung shut behind them and they found themselves in a small courtyard where a group of idle onlookers, a curious and callous crowd, had gathered to stare at this 'God of the Persians' arriving amongst them.

At once they were assaulted by shouts and curses, jeers and taunts. Word had already been spread through the city that these latest arrivals were infidels, sowers of sedition and the worst of criminals. The townspeople had been warned not to associate with them and to treat them with hostility and contempt. But amongst that hostile crowd were one or two individuals upon whom the majesty and dignity of Bahá'u'lláh's presence had an immediate and profound effect. They were drawn to Him and later became His followers.

Of His arrival, Bahá'u'lláh Himself later wrote these words:

> Upon Our arrival We were welcomed with banners of light, whereupon the Voice of the Spirit cried out saying: 'Soon will all that dwell on earth be enlisted under these banners.'[1]

Escorted by thirty policemen, the exhausted exiles were

led through the crowded streets, past the police station, past the bazaar and to the walls of the barracks, then up the long stairs and through the eastern gateway into the bleak and forbidding citadel. The stench inside the barracks was so great that Bahíyyih Khánum fainted the moment she entered the building.

That first night Bahá'u'lláh was confined in a filthy room, devoid of any furniture. The rest of the party were crowded into one other room where ten soldiers stood guard over them. It was unbearably hot and sultry. The only water available for washing and drinking was a brackish and disgusting pool in the courtyard. It stank and was so filthy that no one could consider drinking it. No water was brought to them that first night. A little cooked rice was brought but not enough. They begged for water but were refused. There were small children, babies and nursing mothers amongst the party. The effect of thirst upon them was pitiful; the babies cried incessantly. At last, in the morning, water was brought and three loaves, almost inedible, of black and salty bread were allotted to each prisoner.

The next night Bahá'u'lláh and His family were consigned to the upper floor of the north-west wing. The south-west room of that wing, the unglazed windows of which looked towards the sea, was assigned to Bahá'u'lláh. The floor was of mud, there was no furniture and what plaster still remained on the ceiling was falling onto the floor.

Soon after their arrival the Governor of 'Akká called at the barracks on a tour of inspection. His manner was discourteous in the extreme. He threatened to cut off the bread supply altogether if any of the prisoners attempted to escape. So insulting and provocative were his remarks that the young Ḥusayn-i-Áshchí flung back, in Turkish, an equally insolent reply. 'Abdu'l-Bahá promptly slapped him on the face and ordered him to return to his room at once. At that moment the Governor began to realize that he was not dealing with common criminals. He soon consented to change the inedible black bread for a small allowance and permitted four of the prisoners to go out each day, under guard, to buy provisions for the whole party.

Siyyid Muḥammad and his companion Áqá Ján of Kaj-Kuláh, a retired Turkish artillery officer, now a fervent supporter of Mírzá Yaḥyá, spent a few nights at the citadel. They then asked the authorities if they could be moved away from the rest of the party. They were then housed in a small room above the land gate of 'Akká, a vantage point from which they could watch for any Bahá'í pilgrims who might attempt to enter the city.

Three days after their arrival in 'Akká, the terms of the imperial edict banishing Bahá'u'lláh and His companions to 'Akká were read aloud in the principal mosque of the city. These exiles were, the order ran, condemned to perpetual banishment. They were to be kept in the strictest confinement. They were not to associate either with each other or with the local inhabitants.

Within days of their being confined in the citadel sickness broke out among the exiles. It was autumn, a season notorious for its killing fevers. 'Akká was well-known for its infernal climate and unhealthy atmosphere. So poisonous was the air of the city that a bird flying over 'Akká, it was said, would fall down dead from the stench. There was no water source in the city fit for drinking and a very meagre supply of water for washing was given to the prisoners.

Prisoners sent to 'Akká were usually committed there for life. This was not expected to be – and was not normally – long. Half the prisoners died of disease in the appallingly insanitary and unhealthy conditions in which they were kept. Bahá'u'lláh wrote:

Know thou that upon Our arrival at this Spot, We chose to

designate it as the 'Most Great Prison'. Though previously subjected in another land to chains and fetters, We yet refused to call it by that name. Say: Ponder thereon, O ye endued with understanding![2]

Soon all but two of the exiles were sick and nine of the ten guards set to watch over them also fell ill. No doctor was summoned. Malaria and dysentery added to their discomfort and distress. Three of the exiles died, two of them brothers who died in the same night, locked in each other's arms. There was no money available to pay for their burial and the guards demanded money in advance before they would agree to move the bodies. Bahá'u'lláh gave to the guards a small carpet on which He Himself slept, His only remaining article of luxury, to pay for the burial expenses. These guards sold the carpet but kept the money for themselves. The corpses were buried without ceremony, unwashed and unshrouded, outside the Muslim cemetery even though the money obtained from the sale of the carpet was twice the amount necessary to pay for a decent burial.

After the three deaths, Bahá'u'lláh revealed for the remainder of the party a short healing prayer and asked them to chant it repeatedly with the utmost sincerity. Soon all recovered.

The harsh rules laid down by the imperial farmán were at first most strictly applied. If a barber was needed in the prison, a policeman stood by while he worked and conversation was forbidden.

Bahá'u'lláh had undertaken that none of the Bahá'ís would teach their Faith to anyone in 'Akká or the surrounding countryside while they were exiles and prisoners. Such was their isolation during the early months that rumours spread in Persia that Bahá'u'lláh had drowned on his way to 'Akká. Bahá'u'lláh later wrote:

After Our departure from Adrianople, a discussion arose

among the government officials in Constantinople as to whether We and Our companions should be thrown into the sea. The report of such a discussion reached Persia, and gave rise to a rumour that We had actually suffered that fate.[3]

CHAPTER 20

CLOSE CONFINEMENT

SOME months before they had been ordered to leave Adrianople, 'Abdu'l-Bahá had instructed one of the believers, a man named Mírzá 'Abdu'l-Aḥad, to settle in 'Akká. He was not, 'Abdu'l-Bahá impressed upon him, to give anyone reason to suspect him of being a Bahá'í. Mírzá 'Abdu'l-Aḥad followed 'Abdu'l-Bahá's instructions and, with the help of the Persian agent in 'Akka, was able to obtain permission to live in the city and to open a small shop. When Bahá'u'lláh and His companions arrived, he made no attempt to contact them; it would have been far too dangerous.

The terms of the imperial edict were at first so strictly enforced that it was six or seven months before the exiles were able to make contact with Mírzá 'Abdu'l-Aḥad. Those who left the citadel, accompanied by guards, to buy their daily supplies knew that he was a Bahá'í and bought provisions from his store but they could not speak to him openly.

The Bahá'ís of the Iṣfáhán area were so greatly disturbed by the rumour that Bahá'u'lláh had drowned that they made an appeal to the British telegraphic office, recently installed in Julfá, to establish the truth or falsity of this rumour. Word reached Julfá by telegraph that Bahá'u'lláh and His companions were alive and prisoners in 'Akká. Great was the relief and at once a few wealthy believers of Iṣfáhán utilized this same telegraph service to send some money to the exiles. This was most welcome, for the prisoners by this time had exhausted all their own resources. In the meantime, two believers, a husband and wife, travelled all the way from

Persia to discover the truth or falsity of the rumour for themselves. 'Abdu'l-Aḥad hid them in the back of his shop and with considerable difficulty conveyed to Bahá'u'lláh the news of their arrival. So great was the danger that Bahá'u'lláh asked them to leave the city after only three days. There was absolutely no possibility of them seeing Him. Assured and rejoicing, these two devoted souls returned to Persia.

Once word was out that Bahá'u'lláh was alive and a prisoner in 'Akká, one by one, pilgrims set out on foot from Persia and 'Iráq, on the long and exhausting trek across mountains and deserts, unable to restrain their longing to attempt to enter His presence. Shaykh Salmán, too, the courier of Bahá'u'lláh, made his way to 'Akká.

Siyyid Muḥammad and Áqá Ján, securely lodged over the land gate, quickly reported anyone they recognized to the authorities. Nabíl entered 'Akká in October 1868 in disguise but after three days he was recognized and was immediately expelled. He then spent nine months roaming the countryside nearby, living in Nazareth, Haifa, Hebron and Jerusalem. For a while he lived in the cave of Elijah on Mount Carmel and from there would walk for ten miles to a place beyond the walls of 'Akká from which he could gaze at the window of Bahá'u'lláh's cell.

Two believers, one of them named Amín-i-Iláhí, managed to get into 'Akká disguised as Arab traders. A message was conveyed to them that they would be able to catch a glimpse of Bahá'u'lláh at the public bath. The terms of the edict were still in force but the demeanour and conduct of the prisoners were bringing about gradual changes and Bahá'u'lláh was now able to attend the public bath. Strict instructions were conveyed to Amín-i-Iláhí and his companion that they were on no account to give any sign of recognizing Bahá'u'lláh nor attempt to approach Him. But as soon as Amín-i-Iláhí caught sight of Bahá'u'lláh he was so overcome with emotion that his whole body shook. He stumbled and fell, injuring himself severely on the stone floor, and was carried from the bathhouse, bleeding profusely.

In Adrianople, 'Abdu'l-Bahá had begun to act as a shield to Bahá'u'lláh, arranging the affairs of His household, dealing with the demands of the authorities and allowing only those whose search for truth was sincere to obtain access to Bahá'u'lláh's presence. On arriving in 'Akká Bahá'u'lláh decided to devote all of His own time to the needs of the Bahá'ís themelves and to revealing the teachings that would be needed by the world in the coming centuries. This freedom from daily cares and pressures allowed Him the time He needed to set down His teachings.

As the months passed, the harsh severity of the terms of imprisonment were gradually relaxed as a result of the favourable impression created in the minds of the local officials by the words and deeds of 'Abdu'l-Bahá. One of the privileges now granted to the prisoners was that of attending the regular prayer meetings at a mosque near the prison. But still, the few pilgrims entering the city unobserved were unable to attain the presence of Bahá'u'lláh. Some of the arriving pilgrims were men of wealth and learning but they were content to exist outside the city as itinerant pedlars surviving on a pittance earned from selling matches, cotton and needles, solely in order to be near their Beloved. The most that all the pilgrims could hope for was to stand beyond the second moat and from there catch a glimpse of Bahá'u'lláh's hand or of a handkerchief waved from the small barred window of His cell. An elderly pilgrim from Mosul, an uncle of Ḥusayn-i-Áshchí, stood gazing for hours at the fortress; his feeble sight did not permit him to see Bahá'u'lláh wave His own hand in acknowledgement of his presence. Nabíl entered 'Akká for a second time in February and this time managed to stay for a longer period but was once again recognized and expelled.

Despite the severity of the exiles' confinement, despite the fact that He was virtually isolated from all those who believed in His teachings, Bahá'u'lláh confidently assured His followers that the prison gates would open and that His teachings would spread throughout the world.

'Fear not,' He wrote. 'These doors shall be opened, My tent shall be pitched on Mount Carmel, and the utmost joy shall be realized.'[1]

While confined to His cheerless prison cell, He continued the work that He had begun in Adrianople of proclaiming His mission to those who held the reins of authority, the kings and rulers of the world. A second letter to Napoleon III was smuggled out of the prison and conveyed to the king through the local agent of the French government in 'Akká.

'O King of Paris!' Bahá'u'lláh wrote. 'Tell the priest to ring the bells no longer. By God, the True One! The Most Mighty Bell hath appeared in the form of Him Who is the Most Great Name . . .'[2]

In this powerful Tablet, Bahá'u'lláh warns the king that unless he recognizes His Cause, makes amends for his past deeds and arises to serve Him, he will fall from power. Napoleon III met his downfall in 1870.

From the same cell Bahá'u'lláh wrote to the Czar Alexander II: 'O Czar of Russia! Incline thine ear unto the voice of God . . . Beware lest thy sovereignty withhold thee from Him Who is the Supreme Sovereign . . . Arise thou amongst men in the name of this all-compelling Cause, and summon, then, the nations unto God, the Exalted, the Great.'[3]

In 1881 the Czar was assassinated and in 1917 his dynasty was overthrown.

In a letter to Queen Victoria, Bahá'u'lláh admonishes the queen to 'Cast away all that is on earth, and attire the head of thy kingdom with the crown of the remembrance of thy Lord . . .'[4]

Bahá'u'lláh commends the British queen for abolishing trade in slaves and for entrusting 'the reins of counsel into the hands of the representatives of the people' but warns that those representatives must be trustworthy and must 'regard themselves as the representatives of all that dwell on earth'.[5]

In a majestic Tablet addressed to Pope Pius IX, Bahá'u'lláh addresses the pontiff in these words:

> O Pope! Rend the veils asunder. He Who is the Lord of Lords is come overshadowed with clouds, and the decree hath been fulfilled by God, the Almighty, the Unrestrained . . . He, verily, hath again come down from Heaven even as He came down from it the first time. Beware that thou dispute not with Him even as the Pharisees disputed with Him (Jesus) without a clear token or proof.[6]

In 1870 the Pope's temporal power was severely curtailed when King Victor Emmanuel of Italy went to war with the Papal states.

Bahá'u'lláh had, while in Adrianople, revealed a long and stirring Tablet for Náṣiri'd-Dín Sháh, who had imprisoned and then exiled Him. A number of believers longed for the honour of carrying this Tablet to the Sháh but Bahá'u'lláh waited. The person who would be worthy and able to carry out this difficult mission, He told them, had not yet arrived.

Then, in early 1869, a pilgrim youth, only seventeen years old, slipped into the city dressed as a water-carrier. His name was Áqá Buzurg and he was the son of Ḥájí 'Abdu'l-Majíd, a noted merchant of Níshápúr and a survivor of the grim struggle of Shaykh Ṭabarsí. The Ḥájí had for years despaired of his wild and unruly son who remained aloof and indifferent to the Faith he himself had espoused.

Áqá Buzurg was the despair of his entire family until, one day, Nabíl-i-A'ẓam visited Níshápúr and stayed at the home of 'Abdu'l-Majíd. Surprised that the merchant himself attended to all his needs, Nabíl enquired after the merchant's son and was told of his unruly life and disrespect for his father. Nabíl later recounted: 'I said, "Send for him to come, I wish to see him." He was sent for and he came. I saw a tall, gangling youth, who, instead of physical perfections, had merely a simple heart, and I told his father to make him my host and leave his case to God . . . Then, I mentioned matters, very moving, which would melt a heart of stone.'

That evening Áqá Buzurg's soul was set ablaze. Hearing of the sufferings of the Báb and Bahá'u'lláh he wept aloud.

'I calmed his agitation,' Nabíl recounts, 'but throughout that night, his enamourment and attraction kept sleep away from the eyes . . . Until the light broke we read and recited from the holy script.'[7]

Áqá Buzurg begged to be allowed to go with Nabíl to Mashhad but complied with his father's wish that he remain at home, learn to read and write and then study and make a copy of the *Kitáb-i-Íqán*. Later he travelled with another believer to Yazd and from there he set out alone, on foot, for Baghdád. Soon after his arrival in Baghdád, Áqá 'Abdu'r-Rasúl, who carried water to the believers, was brutally murdered. Áqá Buzurg took his place. Then the believers were rounded up, in preparation for their exile to Mosul. Áqá Buzurg was wounded but escaped from Baghdád and headed for Mosul. When the believers arrived there, he once again served them as a water-carrier.

Consumed with longing to attain the presence of Bahá'u'lláh, Áqá Buzurg left Mosul and walked to 'Akká. Still dressed as a humble water-carrier, he had no problem entering the city but then had no idea how to proceed. He was hungry, footsore, lonely and heartsore, so near and yet so far from his cherished goal. Attending a mosque to pray for guidance, he caught sight of a group of Persians, 'Abdu'l-Bahá amongst them. When the time of prayer was over, he approached 'Abdu'l-Bahá and reverently handed him a note. He had written, on the spot, a few lines of poetry in which he declared his faith in Bahá'u'lláh. That same night, 'Abdu'l-Bahá, with difficulty, arranged for him to enter the citadel.

Twice Áqá Buzurg was ushered alone into the presence of Bahá'u'lláh. In those two interviews he was, in the words of Bahá'u'lláh, 'created anew'. Bahá'u'lláh bestowed upon him a new name 'Badí'', the Wonderful, and in answer to his request, gave to him the mission of delivering the Tablet which He had revealed for Náṣiri'd-Dín Sháh.

Badí' knew, as did the other believers, that whoever took this Tablet to the Sháh would probably yield up his life and that such a mission could bring to peril to all the believers in Persia. For this reason, Bahá'u'lláh instructed Badí' that he must travel alone and avoid contact with any of the Bahá'ís living in Persia. He was told to go to Haifa and wait there for the Tablet to be delivered to him.

Badí' went to wait in Haifa as instructed. A believer named Ḥájí Sháh-Muḥammad was instructed to meet him there. Ḥájí Sháh-Muḥammad later recounted:

> I was given a small case . . . and was instructed to hand it to Badí' at Haifa together with a small sum of money. I did not know anything about the contents of the case. I met him at Haifa and gave him the glad-tidings that he had been honoured with a trust . . . We left the town and walked up Mount Carmel where I handed him the case. He took it into his hands, kissed it and knelt with his forehead to the ground. I also delivered to him a sealed envelope. He took twenty or thirty paces, sat down facing the most Holy Court ['Akká], read the Tablet and again prostrated himself to the ground. His face was illumined with the radiance of ecstasy and the tidings of joy. I asked him if I could read the Tablet also. He replied: 'There is no time.' I knew it was all a confidential matter. But what it was, I had no idea. I could not imagine such a mission.
>
> I mentioned that we had better go to the town in order that, as instructed, I might give him some money. He said, 'I will not come to the town; you go and bring it here.' I went; when

I returned I could not find him, in spite of much searching. He had gone . . .[8]

Alone, and by a roundabout route, Badí' made his way towards Persia. At Trebizond he met with a Bahá'í named Hájí 'Alí who travelled with him towards the Persian frontier and who later recalled:

> He was a very happy person, smiling, patient, thankful, gentle and humble. All that we knew about him was that he had attained the presence of Bahá'u'lláh and was now returning to his home in Khurásán. Many a time he could be seen walking about a hundred feet from the road in either direction, turning his face towards 'Akká, prostrating himself to the ground saying: 'O God! do not take back through Thy justice what thou hast vouchsafed unto me through Thy bounty and grant me strength for its protection.[9]

Badí' reached Ṭihrán but made no contact with the believers; even his own father had no idea that his son was back in the country. His journey on foot from 'Akká had taken over three months. Learning that the Sháh was on a hunting trip at his summer resort of Lár, Badí' went straight there. There he waited, on a rock within sight of the royal pavilion. For three days he prayed and fasted, waiting for the Sháh's hunting party to pass. On the fourth day the Sháh, looking through his binoculars, noticed him and from his motionless, respectful attitude guessed that he wished to make a petition. The Sháh sent a few of his men to find out what Badí' wanted. Badí' told them that he had a letter for the king which he must deliver personally. Surprisingly, the officers allowed him to keep the letter and escorted him to the king. Face to face with the Sháh, Badí' courteously handed over the letter, quoting as he did so the well-known verse from the Qur'án, 'O King, I have come unto thee from Sheba with a weighty message.'[10]

The king immediately ordered his arrest. The letter was

sent at once to a renowned divine in Ṭihrán and a response was requested. The Sháh ordered his men to obtain from Badí', by persuasion or any other means, the names of other Bahá'ís in Persia. Badí' revealed no names. He was beaten until the half-dozen men set to beat him were worn out but still he did not speak. Then his clothes were stripped from him and he was branded with red-hot irons. He was tortured in this manner for three successive days. Still he did not say anything though the smoke and stench of his burning flesh drove several officials out of the tent where he was held. Badí' was joyous throughout the ordeal. He did not appear to be feeling the pain but smiled and laughed often. The officials were helpless but the Sháh insisted that they make Badí' confess and then kill him. The officer in charge, infuriated when Badí' laughed yet again after the branding irons were used another time, lost his temper and ordered that Badí' be put to death. His head was beaten to a pulp and his body thrown into a pit. Earth and stones were heaped over it.

The divines of Ṭihrán had no answer for the letter. There was, they said, nothing to answer. 'If, God forbid,' the chief of their group wrote in reply, 'you should have any doubts regarding Islám and your belief is not firm enough, I ought to take action to dispel your doubts. Otherwise such letters have no answer. The answer was exactly what you did to his messenger. Now you must write to the Ottoman Sulṭán to be very strict with him and prevent all communications.'[11]

The Sháh was, reportedly, most displeased with this reply but could not persuade the divines to write an answer to Bahá'u'lláh. Káẓim Khan, the official who ordered the death of Badí', went mad just eighteen months later. The Sháh ordered that he be chained up and he died a miserable death.

CHAPTER 21

THE PRISON DOORS OPEN

WHEN the news of Badí's death reached 'Akká, Bahá'u'lláh lamented his sufferings and praised his courage and constancy. In almost every Tablet revealed over the next three years, He glorified the station of Badí', calling him 'The Pride of Martyrs' and the 'Salt of My Tablets'.

Badí' was killed in July 1869. Orders were sent at once to the Persian Ambassador in Constantinople. He was to make certain that Bahá'u'lláh remained in the strictest possible confinement. In September, two months after Badí' was killed and a little over a year after Bahá'u'lláh's arrival in 'Akká, the Ambassador wrote to his government:

> I have issued telegraphic and written instructions, forbidding that He (Bahá'u'lláh) associate with any one except His wives and children, or leave under any circumstances, the house wherein He is imprisoned. 'Abbás-Qulí Khán, the Consul-General in Damascus . . . I have, three days ago, sent back, instructing him to proceed direct to 'Akká . . . confer with its governor regarding all necessary measures for the strict maintenance of their imprisonment . . . and appoint, before his return to Damascus, a representative on the spot to insure that the orders issued by the Sublime Porte, will, in no wise, be disobeyed. I have, likewise, instructed him that once every three months he should proceed from Damascus to 'Akká and personally watch over them, and submit his report to the Legation.[1]

The Ottoman authorities did all that they could to keep events under their strictest control but the officials in 'Akká who were directly responsible for enforcing the terms of the edict became less and less willing to carry them out. However, Bahá'u'lláh remained a prisoner and very few pilgrims who reached 'Akká were able to attain to His presence. So the second year of imprisonment went by. Then, in late June, came tragedy.

Mírzá Mihdí, the Purest Branch, Bahá'u'lláh's second surviving son, a full brother of 'Abdu'l-Bahá, had been a very small child when Bahá'u'lláh was exiled from Persia. His health, as an infant, was delicate, and his parents had dared not risk exposing him to the hazard of a midwinter journey. For this reason he was left behind in Ṭihrán with his maternal grandmother. A sensitive child of sweet and generous disposition, he had felt intensely the anguish of separation from his parents, his brother and sister through seven years of his early childhood.

Around the year 1860 he was taken to Baghdád and reunited with his parents and the rest of his family. At once he was overwhelmed by the breezes of the new Revelation. From that time he dedicated every moment of his life to his Father. He was renowned for his meekness and for the loving spirit of service which he demonstrated in his daily life. In 'Akká he often acted as an amanuensis to Bahá'u'lláh.

One hot June day in the early evening, Bahá'u'lláh told him that his services would no longer be needed for the time being. Mírzá Mihdí was not feeling very well; several of the family had been unwell and the heat in the prison was oppressive. Bahá'u'lláh suggested that he could go up on the roof of the prison to get some fresh air and to pray and meditate. This he had often done.

That evening, as he paced the roof, absorbed in prayer, he miscounted the steps he was used to taking in that familiar space and fell through an open skylight onto a wooden crate in the room below. The crash of his fall brought the believers running. They found him terribly injured. Blood was pouring from his mouth and the only way they could remove his clothes in order to examine his wounds was to tear them from him.

A physician was called but pronounced his case hopeless. 'Abdu'l-Bahá, with tearful eyes, knelt and begged Bahá'u-'lláh to save His brother's life. 'O My Greatest Branch,' Bahá'u'lláh is reported to have said, 'leave him in the hands of God.'[2]

Dismissing everyone else, Bahá'u'lláh remained with His dying son, showering upon him His bounties and favour. As his end drew near others came to the bedside. 'What do you wish, tell Me,' Bahá'u'lláh asked His son. Mírzá Mihdí replied, 'I wish the people of Bahá to be able to attain Your presence.' 'And so it shall be, God will grant your wish,' Bahá'u'lláh answered.[3]

Twenty-two hours after his fall, Mírzá Mihdí passed away. Bahá'u'lláh was heard lamenting aloud, 'Mihdí! O Mihdí!'[4] His mother was overwhelmed by the loss of this youngest, precious son, from whom she had already been separated for so many years. She wept unceasingly until her family feared for her reason. She was only comforted when Bahá'u'lláh assured her that her son had willingly given his life as a ransom for the quickening of all mankind.

One of the leading religious leaders of 'Akká, Shaykh Maḥmúd, begged for the privilege of washing and shrouding the body of the Purest Branch. Shaykh Maḥmúd, formerly renowned for the fanatical narrowness of his views, had once sought to end Bahá'u'lláh's life with his own dagger but had instead become a believer. His request was granted and a tent was pitched in the prison yard. The body of the Purest Branch was washed in the presence of Bahá'u'lláh, was carried respectfully from the citadel and laid to rest in a graveyard outside the city walls. The notables of 'Akká filed behind the casket in the funeral procession as a sign of their respect for Bahá'u'lláh and His family. At the time that the exiles returned to the barracks an earth tremor shook the area.

In a prayer revealed for His son at the time of his death, Bahá'u'lláh wrote:

> Glorified art Thou, O Lord, my God! Thou seest me in the hands of Mine enemies, and My son bloodstained before Thy face, O Thou in Whose hands is the kingdom of all names. I have, O my Lord, offered up that which Thou hast given Me, that Thy servants may be quickened and all that dwell on earth be united.[5]

And in another Tablet He has written:

> Erelong will God reveal through thee that which He hath desired. He, verily, is the Truth, the Knower of things unseen. When thou was laid to rest in the earth, the earth itself trembled in its longing to meet thee. Thus hath it been decreed, and yet the people perceive not . . . Were We to recount the mysteries of thine ascension, they that are asleep would waken, and all beings would be set ablaze with the fire of the remembrance of My Name, the Mighty, the Loving.[6]

Mírzá Mihdí passed away on 23 June 1870. He was twenty-two years old. Soon after his death many of the irksome restrictions of prison life were relaxed and several of the believers who had come as pilgrims were able to enter the presence of Bahá'u'lláh. Then, four months later, in October 1870, the Ottoman authorities required the barracks to house troops. Bahá'u'lláh protested that the exiles should not be crowded in with the soldiers. The Governor, who by this time had become less hostile, agreed to let Bahá'u'lláh, His family and companions leave the citadel and live in a small house in 'Akká.

'How we rejoiced in our liberty, restricted though it was,' Bahíyyih Khánum later recalled. 'Only three times had we been permitted to go out, for even an hour, from the prison barracks during the whole of that first two years.

'How tired we were of those three little rooms!'[7]

CHAPTER 22

A FRESH DANGER

Most of the exiles were moved to the Khan-i-'Avámíd, a caravanserai which was in a bad state of disrepair. The rooms available to them were damp and filthy. Food was scarce; individual beans were counted out and allotted to each person and each loaf of bread available was divided into very small portions. Mírzá Músá managed to rent a house within the compound of the caravanserai and a few others found separate homes. Bahá'u'lláh and His family were accommodated wherever space could be found for them. First they were moved from the prison to the house of Malik in the western part of the city. After three months in that house they were moved to the house opposite, the house of Manṣúr Khavvám. Here again, their stay was short. Another move saw them in the house of Rábi'ih. But this house too was only available for a limited period and after four months they moved to cramped quarters in the house of 'Údí Khammár near to the sea wall.

'Údí Khammár was a wealthy merchant and a Maronite Christian. He was well-known in 'Akká for his parsimony and it was therefore a considerable surprise to all when he decided to build a palatial mansion at Bahjí, a short distance outside 'Akká. He moved there, leasing his town house to Bahá'u'lláh.

'Údí Khammár, an individual of wealth and influence in 'Akká, was not particularly well-disposed towards his new tenants. He had listened to all the ugly lies which had been spread through the city when the exiles arrived and had believed them. His relative, Ilyás 'Abbúd, whose house adjoined the house of ‘Údí Khammár, was decidedly hostile. When he heard of his relative’s plan, he tried to prevent Bahá’u’lláh from renting the house, but failed. However, he took every possible step to avoid contact with his new neighbours, whom he considered highly undesirable.

The ground floors of both houses were used as business premises. ‘Údí Khammár’s was the smaller of the two houses and faced away from the sea. Its living quarters were totally inadequate for the needs of Bahá’u’lláh’s family. Thirteen people of both sexes had to share one small room where one person was obliged to sleep on a narrow shelf high on the wall. ‘Abdu’l-Bahá went to live in the Khán-i-‘Avámíd.

Release from the prison quarters did not bring relief from harassment and abuse. Although the few important officials charged with carrying out the Sulṭán’s orders were now beginning to change their antagonistic attitudes and although the guards who had attended the exiles closely for two years were now dismissed, the general populace was still deeply hostile towards the Bahá’ís. The minds of the majority of the people were still poisoned with the lies they had been fed when the exiles first arrived. The Bahá’ís were still regarded by the mass of the ordinary people as dangerous heretics, renegades against the true Faith, traitors, outlaws and licentious ruffians. Now, when it seemed that, at last, things might take a turn for the better, a fresh danger arose from the activities of the Azalís, the followers of Mírzá Yaḥyá, in ‘Akká.

Siyyid Muḥammad and Áqá Ján, firmly settled into their quarters above the land gate, continued to do all in their power to prevent any pilgrims entering the city and to damage the reputation of the Bahá’ís. They were joined at this stage by Mírzá Riḍá-Qulí, a brother-in-law of Mírzá Yaḥyá, and his sister, Badrí-Ján, the estranged wife of Mírzá

Yaḥyá. Mírzá Riḍá-Qulí had behaved in public so badly so often and had brought such public disgrace upon all the believers that Bahá'u'lláh had expelled him from the community.

The campaign of lies, of abuse, of intrigue and misrepresentation put about by the Azalís and their new recruit now rose to vicious heights. Time and again they carried fresh slanders against the Bahá'ís to the authorities. Time and again 'Abdu'l-Bahá's words and deeds acted as an antidote to those poisonous tales. With each failure to blacken the name of the Bahá'ís, the Azalís became more desperately determined to harm them. The populace was roused to open enmity against the Bahá'ís. The situation became extremely fraught and so perilous that Bahá'u'lláh's own life was in peril. An added complication was the fact that the Persian consular agent had fallen deeply under the influence of the Azalís.

Bahá'u'lláh repeatedly counselled His faithful followers to patience and forbearance. Some of the believers, driven to distraction by the constant and ever-increasing harassment, begged Bahá'u'lláh to allow them to deal with the mischief-makers in their own way. One Arab believer named Náṣir came from Beirut intent on personally silencing the trouble-makers. Once his intention became clear, Bahá'u'lláh immediately ordered him back to Beirut.

Bahá'u'lláh categorically forbade His followers to entertain any thought of violence or retaliation but some of those He counselled chose to ignore that command. They knew that Bahá'u'lláh would condemn their action in the strongest possible terms but they could not bear to see Him so mercilessly slandered. They therefore began to plot as to how they could rid themselves of their persecutors.

Once again, as in 'Iráq and later in Adrianople, Bahá'u'lláh secluded Himself from all. 'Abdu'l-Bahá moved from the caravanserai and stayed close to Him in the house of ‘Údí Khammár. Siyyid Muḥammad and his associates took fresh advantage of this seclusion. Siyyid Muḥammad wrote letters to Persia relating that Bahá’u’lláh had cut off all association with His followers. Mírzá Riḍá-Qulí had in his possession some writings of Bahá’u’lláh. These he cunningly falsified, adding passages designed to arouse the venom of the credulous and prejudiced populace. The agony which Bahá’u’lláh experienced can be glimpsed in the verses of *The Fire Tablet*, which He revealed at this time:

> The necks of men are stretched out in malice . . . The whisperings of Satan have been breathed to every creature . . . Bahá is drowning in a sea of tribulation . . . The lamps of truth and purity, of loyalty and honour have been put out . . . This Face is hidden in the dust of slander: Where are the breezes of Thy compassion, O Mercy of the worlds?[1]

Soon after this, on 21 January 1872 Bahá’u’lláh revealed another Tablet foreshadowing the imminent appearance of a catastrophe which would crash, like a great wave, on the community.

The next day seven of Bahá’u’lláh’s own companions armed themselves and killed Siyyid Muḥammad, Áqá Ján and Mírzá Riḍá-Qulí. The sound of shots near the Seraye brought the Governor himself out of his house. The city erupted in anger and protest.

‘All,’ Áqá Riḍá relates, ‘young and old, notables and humble folk, the Governor, the Chief of Police, and troops rose up, as if a powerful state had made an attack on them. Armed with stones and sticks, swords and rifles, they set out towards the house of the Blessed Perfection and the houses of the companions, arresting whomever they met.’[2]

Troops, their swords drawn, surrounded the house of ‘Údí Khammár and the clamour of an angry crowd was heard on all sides. An hour after sunset an army officer, accompanied by Ilyás ‘Abbúd, entered the house. Bahá’u’lláh and a number of believers, 'Abdu'l-Bahá amongst them, were summoned to the government headquarters.

By the light of a lantern, Bahá'u'lláh, 'Abdu'l-Bahá and the other believers were escorted to the Seraye. Such was the majesty of Bahá'u'lláh's appearance on that night that one citizen of 'Akká who saw Him then instantly believed Him and became His loyal follower. When Bahá'u'lláh entered the Seraye the entire body of officials waiting to accuse Him stood up before Him. In utter silence, Bahá'u'lláh walked to the top end of the room and took a seat there. Only then did the garrison commandant speak:

'It is proper', he asked, 'that some of your followers should act in such a manner?'

Bahá'u'lláh replied, 'If one of your soldiers were to commit a reprehensible act, would you be held responsible, and be punished in his place?'

Four hours later Bahá'u'lláh was escorted to a room in a nearby caravanserai and was kept there in custody with one of His sons for the night. 'Abdu'l-Bahá was put in the prison in chains for one night and was then transferred to the caravanserai. Twenty-five of Bahá'u'lláh's followers were also thrown into gaol. That first night the whole town was in turmoil. A Russian steamer arrived before 'Akká that same night and the officials forbade anyone to leave either the ship or the city. The Governor cabled an account of the steps he had taken to his superior in Damascus, Ṣubḥí Pásh̲á, the Válí of Syria. The Válí cabled back a reprimand. He was most displeased with the treatment given to Bahá'u'lláh.

The next day Bahá'u'lláh was moved to better quarters above the prison. On the afternoon of the third day He was summoned again to the Seraye. Shoghi Effendi has given us an account of this interview. His description is based on details which Bahá'u'lláh dictated to His amanuensis, Mírzá Áqá Ján.

When interrogated, He was asked to state His name and that of the country from which He came. 'It is more manifest than the sun,' He answered. The same question was put to Him again, to which He gave the following reply: 'I deem it not proper to mention it. Refer to the farmán of the goverment which is in your possession.' Once again they, with marked deference, reiterated their request, whereupon Bahá'u'lláh spoke with majesty and power these words: 'My name is Bahá'u'lláh (Light of God), and My country in Núr (Light). Be ye apprized of it.' Turning then, to the Muftí, He addressed him words of veiled rebuke, after which He spoke to the entire gathering, in such vehement and exalted language that none made bold to answer Him. Having quoted verses from the Súriy-i-Mulúk, He, afterwards, arose and left the gathering. The Governor, soon after, sent word that He was at liberty to return to His home, and apologized for what had occurred.[3]

The seven who were guilty of the murders were kept in prison for seven years. Sixteen other believers were put under guard in the caravanserai and were kept there, in the same room in which Bahá'u'lláh had been held on that first night, for the next six months.

The damage caused by this incident was severe. 'Were We', Bahá'u'lláh wrote shorty after the murders took place, 'to make mention of what befell Us, the heavens would be rent asunder and the mountains would crumble.'[4]

The believers were reviled and openly cursed in the streets. Their children, when they dared to appear in the open, were abused and pelted with stones. Ilyás 'Abbúd, now thoroughly alarmed, reinforced the walls of his house where they adjoined the house of his relative, barricading himself off from any possible access to the Bahá'ís. Once again, severe restrictions were imposed on the exiles and pilgrims were unable to enter the city. Bahá'u'lláh remained confined in the house of 'Údí Khammár.

CHAPTER 23
THE TURNING TIDE

In the Síyáh-Chál in Ṭihrán and in His exile from His homeland, Bahá'u'lláh had endured the onslaughts of external enemies. In Adrianople the severest test ever to befall the infant Faith had been an internal one. This time, in 'Akká, the assault was threefold, from the Ottoman authorities, from the Azalís and from the misguided followers of Bahá'u'lláh Himself.

It was the latter group, His own disobedient followers, who caused Bahá'u'lláh the most anguish. 'My captivity', He wrote, 'cannot harm Me. That which can harm Me is the conduct of those who love Me, who claim to be related to Me, and yet perpetrate what causeth My heart and My pen to groan.'[1]

This mental anguish, combined with the physical weakness resulting from two years in the Most Great Prison, took a severe toll.

'Because of His physical weakness,' 'Abdu'l-Bahá later wrote, 'brought on by His afflictions, His blessed body was worn away to a breath; it was light as a cobweb from long grieving.'[2]

Yet, at this critical hour, when the actions of His own followers had brought such danger upon all the believers, when the fear and hatred felt by the general populace in 'Akká had reached to a new pitch of intensity, and when Bahá'u'lláh Himself was still in frail health, slowly and gradually the light of the new Revelation began to shine in 'Akká with a new strength and brilliance. In the early months of 1873, one year after the murder of the Azalís, while troubles still surged about Him, Bahá'u'lláh began to reveal the *Kitáb-i-Aqdas*, His Book of Laws.

In the *Kitáb-i-Aqdas*, the Most Holy Book of the Bahá'í era, Bahá'u'lláh abrogates the laws of the Báb, confirming only a few of those laws which the Báb had revealed in the Bayán, and gives to His followers the laws of the Bahá'í dispensation. However, when the *Kitáb-i-Aqdas* was completed and shared with the believers, Bahá'u'lláh counselled those followers who were with Him in 'Akká and the believers elsewhere that not all these new laws would be adopted immediately. Some of them would be adopted gradually, stage by stage, as the world acquired the necessary maturity.

Bahá'u'lláh Himself describes this book in these words:

> Verily, it is My weightiest testimony unto all people, and the proof of the All-Merciful unto all who are in heaven and all who are on earth . . . So vast is its range that it hath encompassed all men ere their recognition of it. Erelong will its sovereign power, its pervasive influence and the greatness of its might be manifested on earth.[3]

Shoghi Effendi has summarized its importance in these words:

> . . . this Book, this treasury enshrining the priceless gems of His Revelation, stands out, by virtue of the principles it inculcates, the administrative institutions it ordains and the function with which it invests the appointed Successor of its Author, unique and incomparable among the world's sacred Scriptures.[4]

In the *Kitab-i-Aqdas* Bahá'u'lláh completes His summons to the kings and rulers of the world, a summons which Shoghi Effendi describes as:

> . . . a summons which stands unparalleled in the annals of any previous religion, and to which the messages directed by the Prophet of Islám to some of the rulers among His contemporaries alone offer a faint resemblance.[5]

Bahá'u'lláh Himself states that, 'Never since the beginning of the world hath the Message been so openly proclaimed.'[6]

He delineates a charter for a new world civilization built upon the principle of the oneness and wholeness of the entire human race. He sets out the basic principles on which such a new stage in human social evolution will be based, including the harmony of science and religion, the equality of men and women, the provision of education for all, the abolition of extremes of wealth and poverty. He outlines the principle of collective security by which the peoples of the world may establish peace and abolish warfare between nations. He repeatedly stresses the necessity for an international auxiliary language and emphasizes the need for genuine consultation between peoples and nations.

Shoghi Effendi has described the revelation of this one book as 'what may well rank as the most signal act' of Bahá'u'lláh's ministry and refers to it as 'the brightest emanation of the mind of Bahá'u'lláh . . . the Mother Book of His Dispensation' and 'the Charter of His New World Order'.[7] The Universal House of Justice has described it as 'the kernal of a vast structure of Bahá'í law that will have to come into being in the years and centuries ahead as the unity of mankind is established and develops'.[8]

In this book the laws given by Bahá'u'lláh to the peoples of the world are interwoven with passages of spiritual counsel and loving exhortation, the whole revealed in prose of matchless beauty.

'O ye peoples of the world!' Bahá'u'lláh writes in the *Kitáb-i-Aqdas*:

> Know assuredly that My commandments are the lamps of My loving providence among My servants, and the keys of My mercy for My creatures . . .
>
> Think not that We have revealed unto you a mere code of laws. Nay, rather, We have unsealed the choice Wine with

> the fingers of might and power . . . Meditate upon this, O men of insight![9]

So potent was the spiritual energy imparted to the world through the actual revelation of this Book that it was in itself a major factor in causing the restrictions which were still in force against the exiles to be significantly eased.

A year after the murder of the Azalís, the Governor of 'Akká, who had remained ill-disposed towards the exiles, was dismissed from office and replaced by Aḥmad Big Tawfíq, a wise and compassionate man. Soon after his installation as Governor, Badrí-Ján, the sister of the murdered Mírzá Riḍá-Qulí, sought an interview with Aḥmad Big Tawfíq and there accused Bahá'u'lláh of instigating the murders and of plotting to rule over all, the kings of the world included. To back up her allegations, she left with the Governor a copy of the *Súriy-i-Mulúk* and some other writings of Bahá'u'lláh.

Badrí-Ján's efforts backfired. The Governor was so impressed by these writings that he sought out 'Abdu'l-Bahá in order to learn more. So captivated was he by the demeanour and wisdom of 'Abdu'l-Bahá that he, the Governor of the city, would reverently shed his shoes when in the presence of 'Abdu'l-Bahá. He asked that all the writings of Bahá'u'lláh already in his possession be copied for him in exquisite calligraphy and he repeatedly requested the honour of an interview with Bahá'u'lláh. He also began to send his own son to 'Abdu'l-Bahá for instruction and it was rumoured that he himself sought the counsel of the exiles in matters relating to the governing of the city.

Ilyás 'Abbúd, too, began to change his hostile attitude towards his immediate neighbours. Here again the change was brought about by his contacts with 'Abdu'l-Bahá. After a while, he knocked down the barricade he had so hastily erected, in the aftermath of the murder of the Azalís, between his house and the house of 'Údí K̲h̲ammár. In the spring of 1872, when Munírih K̲h̲ánum arrived in 'Akká as the prospective bride of 'Abdu'l-Bahá, Ilyás 'Abbúd himself waited with Mírzá Músá at the harbour of 'Akká to welcome her and brought her into the city as his own guest. This was at a time when no other Bahá'ís were able to enter 'Akká.

It was as a result of the repeated requests made by Ilyás 'Abbúd that Bahá'u'lláh consented to receive Aḥmad Big Tawfíq. In this interview Bahá'u'lláh requested the Governor to review the cases of the Bahá'ís who were held in captivity. The Governor agreed and carefully reviewed each case. All those except the seven responsible for the murders were released in July of 1873.

In this same interview the Governor asked to be allowed to present a gift or perform some service for Bahá'u'lláh. Bahá'u'lláh gently refused the offer of a personal gift but asked the Governor to rebuild a ruined aqueduct so that fresh water could be brought into 'Akká for all its citizens. This aqueduct had been in a state of disrepair for thirty years. Aḥmad Big Tawfíq at once consented to the suggestion and promptly arranged for the work to be done. He also allowed pilgrims to enter the city although their entrance was still officially forbidden.

Munírih K̲h̲ánum stayed for five months with the family of Mírzá Músá. Plans for her marriage to 'Abdu'l-Bahá could not go forward as there was no space available for them in the house of 'Údí K̲h̲ammár. In September, when Ilyás 'Abbúd suddenly realized the reason for the delay, he at once offered a room in his own house and had it beautifully decorated for 'Abdu'l-Bahá and his bride. The marriage took place without further delay.

By January of 1874 the stress and dangers of the dark days following on the murder of the Azalís were fast receding. Then Ilyás 'Abbúd, by now a devoted admirer of Bahá'u-'lláh, fell ill and moved out of 'Akká, renting his town house to the exiles. The entire partition between the two houses was taken down and Bahá'u'lláh moved into a pleasant room facing the sea. There was a veranda too, overlooking the street and the ocean beyond. Here Bahá'u'lláh, who for years had only been able to pace monotonously the floor of His small rooms in the Most Great Prison and in the house of Údí Khammár, was able to enjoy the fresh air and the sea breezes.

The believers living in 'Akká, now about a hundred in number, would leave their shops and businesses before sunset to assemble in the street outside the house of 'Abbúd and often Bahá'u'lláh would summon a few of them to His presence. One of them, Mírzá Muḥammad Ḥádí, a noted binder and illuminator of books, took it upon himself to keep the ground in front of the house free of dirt and refuse. 'Abdu'l-Bahá relates:

> Through his constant efforts, the square in front of Bahá'u'lláh's house was at all times swept, sprinkled and immaculate.
>
> Bahá'u'lláh would often glance at that plot of ground, and then He would smile and say: 'Muḥammad-Ḥádí has turned the square in front of this prison into the bridal-bower of a palace. He has brought pleasure to all the neighbours and earned their thanks.'[10]

Aḥmad Big Tawfíq's term as Governor ended in February 1875 when he was transferred to another post. The new Governor, 'Abdu'r-Raḥmán Páshá, was outwardly friendly towards the Bahá'ís but secretly schemed with those who sought to harm Bahá'u'lláh and His followers. He reported continually to Beirut that the exiles were enjoying considerable freedom to meet whoever they wanted and to run profitable businesses, privileges strictly denied to them in the edict of banishment.

At last the orders he sought arrived from Beirut: he

received permission to close down the shops run by the Bahá'ís. Having succeeded thus far, 'Abdu'r-Raḥmán sought to carry out his objective dramatically. He planned to bring public disgrace and humiliation on the Bahá'ís and to this end he paraded with all pomp and ceremony into the bazaar with a number of lesser officials, only to find that the shops owned by the Bahá'ís were already shut. Bahá'u'lláh had ordered the believers to stay at home on that day. The Governor waited for an hour or two in the home of a sentry, believing that the Bahá'ís would shortly appear. But instead it was the Muftí of 'Akká who appeared, in some consternation, carrying with him a cable from Damascus ordering the dismissal of the Governor.

A rapid succession of Governors followed over the next few years, most of whom showed goodwill towards the exiles but even those who were ill-disposed towards them could not check the turning tide of opinion. Many of the leading citizens of 'Akká now showed the utmost respect and devotion to Bahá'u'lláh. Amongst them was the commandant of the barracks, Colonel Aḥmad-i-Jarráḥ. He had first glimpsed the majesty and dignity of Bahá'u'lláh in the barracks. Then, as an officer detailed to be present when Bahá'u'lláh was brought before the Governor after the murder of the Azalís, he had been deeply moved by the demeanour and the majestic words spoken by Bahá'u'lláh on that occasion. Now he sought out the Bahá'ís, asked for some of Bahá'u'lláh's writings and became a devoted believer.

In May of 1876, Sulṭán 'Abdu'l-'Azíz, who had ordered the imprisonment of Bahá'u'lláh in 'Akká, was deposed on grounds of incapacity and extravagance. Four days after he was removed from his palace, he was found dead. Apparently assassinated, nineteen physicians of Constantinople, men of many nationalities, testified that he had killed himself.

High officials now sought audiences with Bahá'u'lláh but He very seldom agreed to see anyone but the believers. The general populace, who had once been summoned to jeer at Him, now spoke of Him with reverence as 'the august leader' or 'his highness'.[11] He was credited with improving not only the water but the very climate of the city which underwent a noticeable improvement in those years.

Another Governor, Muṣṭafá Ḍíyá Pá<u>sh</u>á, was so deeply impressed by Bahá'u'lláh that he indicated that He might, if He so wished, leave 'Akká for the countryside. Bahá'u'lláh did not avail Himself of this opportunity but one day, He remarked, 'I have not gazed on verdure for nine years. The country is the world of the soul; the city is the world of bodies.'[12]

When 'Abdu'l-Bahá heard of this, He realized that Bahá'u'lláh was longing for the countryside and felt assured that the time had come when arrangements could be made for Him to leave 'Akká. He rented the palace of Mazra'ih, a lovely place some four miles north of 'Akká, from a relative of 'Abdu'lláh Pá<u>sh</u>á and arranged for repairs to be carried out there and a bath to be built. When all was ready, 'Abdu'l-Bahá writes:

> One day I went to the Holy Presence of the Blessed Beauty and said: 'The palace of Mazra'ih is ready for you, and a carriage to drive you there'. He refused to go, saying: 'I am a prisoner.' Later I requested Him again, but got the same answer. I went so far as to ask Him a third time, but He still said 'No!' and I did not dare insist further. There was, however, in 'Akká, a certain Muḥammadan <u>Sh</u>ay<u>kh</u>, a well-known man with considerable influence, who loved Bahá'u-'lláh and was greatly favoured by Him. I called this <u>Sh</u>ay<u>kh</u> and explained the position to him. I said, 'You are daring. Go tonight to His Holy Presence, fall on your knees before Him, take hold of His hands and do not let go until He promises to leave the city!' . . . He went directly to Bahá'u'lláh and sat

down close to His knees. He took hold of the hands of the Blessed Beauty and kissed them and asked: 'Why do you not leave the city?' He said: 'I am a prisoner.' The Shaykh replied: 'God forbid! Who has the power to make you a prisoner? You have kept yourself in prison. It was your own will to be imprisoned, and now I beg you to come out and go to the palace. It is beautiful and verdant. The trees are lovely, and the oranges like balls of fire!' As often as the Blessed Beauty said: 'I am a prisoner, it cannot be,' the Shaykh took His hands and kissed them. For a whole hour he kept on pleading. At last Bahá'u'lláh said, 'Khaylí khúb (very good)' and the Shaykh's patience and persistence were rewarded . . . In spite of the strict firman of 'Abdu'l-'Azíz which prohibited my meeting or having any intercourse with the Blessed Perfection, I took the carriage the next day and drove with Him to the palace. No one made any objection. I left Him there and returned myself to the city.[13].

CHAPTER 24

MAZRA'IH – A PLACE OF FREEDOM

IT was June of 1877 when Bahá'u'lláh left the house of 'Abbúd and moved with some members of His family to Mazra'ih. 'Abdu'l-Bahá, Bahíyyih Khánum and their mother, Navváb, remained in 'Akká but visited Mazra'ih whenever they could. The pressure of commitments in 'Akká kept 'Abdu'l-Bahá fully occupied but, aside from this, he deliberately stayed away from Bahá'u'lláh as his half-brothers, particularly Mírzá Muḥammad-'Alí, had grown jealous of him. Adib Taherzadeh explains that:

> By staying away from Bahá'u'lláh, Who cherished His eldest Son and extolled His station in glowing terms, 'Abdu'l-Bahá succeeded in somewhat dampening the fire of jealousy which was fiercely burning within their breasts. As well as this, Bahá'u'lláh's own practice over the years was, as far as possible, to keep in His company those who were likely to cause trouble or were inwardly unfaithful to Him, so that He could control their mischief and keep them in check. And now that some freedom was given to Him, Bahá'u'lláh chose to live with those members of His household who would prove, in the end, to be disloyal to His Cause.[1]

Mazra'ih is a lovely place. The house, designed as a simple summer residence, stands in quiet countryside north of 'Akká. To the east it overlooks a wide plain beyond which rise the hills of Galilee: to the west, just half a mile away, lie the blue waters of the Mediterranean. Surrounded by gardens, with a small stream running close by, Mazra'ih is a place of light and happiness. Bahá'u'lláh spent much of the next two years at Mazra'ih, returning to stay in 'Akká from time to time.

The delight of the pilgrims who reached Mazra'ih can scarcely be described. So profound was their joy, so overwhelming their happiness in entering the presence of Bahá'u'lláh outside the prison city, that the very walls of Mazra'ih are charged with the spiritual energy and exhilaration of those meetings. Now, with His permission, the believers were able to hold simple feasts at Mazra'ih and also in the Garden of Na'mayn, renamed by Bahá'u'lláh the Garden of Riḍván. This garden, a short distance from 'Akká, 'Abdu'l-Bahá had rented in 1875, in anticipation of Bahá'u'lláh's release from the prison city.

Many of the pilgrims, knowing of Bahá'u'lláh's deep love of nature and the countryside, carried with them on their long and difficult journeys plants and shrubs for this garden, even a rare white rose which grew in Ṭihrán and which had been one of Bahá'u'lláh's favourite flowers. Travelling on foot across the deserts, mountains and plains where water was often scarce or non-existent, they managed to keep these plants alive, even when they themselves went thirsty.

A shallow stream abundant with fish flowed through the garden and a fountain fed water to all the flower beds that the pilgrims and local believers had painstakingly created. The sound of the splashing fountain, the murmur of the stream, the birdsong, the fragrant scents of many blossoms and herbs, the harmonious variety of colour, the delightful shade of shrub and tree refreshed all who entered there. Beneath the shade of two large mulberry trees Bahá'u'lláh received His guests. 'Abdu'l-Bahá's daughter, Ṭúbá Khánum, who lived in 'Akká with her parents, wrote of that garden:

> Oh the joy of the day when Bahá'u'lláh went to the beautiful Riḍván, which had been prepared for Him with such loving care by the Master, the friends, and the pilgrims! . . . Only

those who were present there could realize in any degree what it meant to be surrounded by such profusion of flowers, their colours and their scents, after the dull walls and unfragrant odours of the prison city.[2]

The move to Mazra'ih was the start of a new stage of relative peace and tranquillity for Bahá'u'lláh, His family and those believers who were settled in the Holy Land. At Mazra'ih, Bahá'u'lláh continued to reveal Tablets imparting spiritual counsel and advice, reaffirming and further elucidating the spiritual principles He had laid down in the *Kitáb-i-Aqdas*.

The visits of pilgrimage to Mazra'ih made by the believers from Persia and elsewhere played a vital part in the nurturing of the community of believers in their home countries. The dissemination of the Tablets of Bahá'u'lláh and the personal accounts of those who had reached Mazra'ih quickened the faith of all the believers. Though nominally still a prisoner, Bahá'u'lláh was able to correspond, with relative ease, with His followers. The need for Bahá'u'lláh's guidance was great, for the believers in Persia were allowed no peace or tranquillity, rather they were continuing to endure severe and prolonged persecution.

Of the decades which had passed since 1852, when the three deranged young Bábís had attempted to assassinate the Sháh and through their actions brought such calamity upon all the believers, Shoghi Effendi writes: 'Though on a far smaller scale than the blood baths which had baptized the birth of the Faith . . . the murderous and horrible acts subsequently perpetrated by an insatiable and unyielding enemy covered as wide a range and were marked by an even greater degree of ferocity.'[3]

Náṣiri'd-Dín Sháh remained implacably hostile to the new Faith and totally committed to its destruction. Unable now to punish Bahá'u'lláh Himself, since He and His family were no longer Persian citizens, he was determined to wipe out the remnants of this heresy from every corner of his realm. He had, for the purposes of internal administration, divided between three of his sons the governorships of all the provinces in the country. Two of these princes, Ẓillu's-Sulṭán, the eldest, and Kámrán Mírzá, the Sháh's favourite son, were fierce rivals for their father's favour. To this end, each tried to outdo the other in hunting down, robbing and killing the Bahá'ís. They were firmly supported and abetted by a number of the leading mujtahids, particularly in Ṭihrán and Iṣfáhán. These powerful religious leaders made every effort to eliminate the movement which they perceived as heretical and a danger to their own leadership.

The Bahá'ís offered no resistance. While the Bábís had, between 1848 and 1851, ably defended themselves when attacked, Bahá'u'lláh, from the early days of exile in Baghdád, had instructed the believers not to offer armed resistance, teaching them that 'it is better to be killed than kill'.[4] The Bahá'ís were obedient to this teaching and in such circumstances the Faith was driven underground. Whenever Bahá'ís were discovered they were imprisoned, robbed, tortured and executed in a variety of barbaric ways. In Mázindarán, in Khurásán, in the cities of Ṭihrán, Iṣfáhán, Shíráz, Zanján, Yazd and Mashhad, and through the length and breadth of Persia, numbers of honest and law-abiding citizens were savagely tortured and murdered.

Despite this persecution, the community of believers expanded steadily, drawing considerable numbers of recruits from the Jewish and Zoroastrian communities of Persia. In addition, new territories were opened to the light of the Bahá'í teachings. It was while Bahá'u'lláh was at Mazra'ih that the devoted and experienced travel-teacher Sulaymán Khán-i-Tunukábání, usually referred to as Jamál Effendi, reached India and began a momentous, ten-year long journey throughout the sub-continent and through Sri Lanka and Burma.

Since the death of Badí', Bahá'u'lláh had advised His followers in Persia to exercise the utmost caution and wisdom but even this counsel could not always protect them. In March of 1879, while Bahá'u'lláh was at Mazra'ih, two devoted Bahá'ís of Iṣfáhán, men of flawless character, widely renowned for their integrity and their prodigious charitable works, were beheaded and their bodies dragged through the city streets. Their deaths were brought about by the Imám-Jum'ih of Iṣfáhán, aided and abetted by the leading mujtahid of the city and the Governor of the province himself, the Ẓillu's-Sulṭán.

One of the pilgrims who reached Mazra'ih and died there was Ḥájí Mullá Mihdíy-i-'Aṭrí, a devoted believer from Yazd whose son and grandson were later martyred. Ḥájí Mullá Mihdí had attained the presence of Bahá'u'lláh in Baghdád and there his soul had caught fire. One day, during the time that Bahá'u'lláh was at Mazra'ih, Ḥájí Mullá Mihdí invited the Bahá'ís of Yazd to a meeting in his house. About two hundred believers attended. No such meeting had ever been held in Yazd. Bahá'í songs and Tablets were chanted in that meeting. The next day the leading mujtahid of Yazd had Ḥájí Mullá Mihdí brutally flogged and thrown out of the city. The Ḥájí, accompanied by his two sons, walked towards 'Akká, teaching their Faith as they went, enduring imprisonment and 'terrible, uncounted hardships'. Eventually they reached Beirut. In that city, 'Abdu'l-Bahá recounts of Ḥájí Mullá Mihdí that:

> . . . ill, restive, his patience gone, he spent some days. His yearning grew, and his agitation was such that weak and sick as he was, he could wait no more.
>
> He set out on foot for the house of Bahá'u'lláh. Because he lacked proper shoes for the journey, his feet were bruised and torn; his sickness worsened; he could hardly move, but still

he went on; somehow he reached the village of Mazra'ih and here, close by the Mansion, he died. His heart found his Well-Beloved One, when he could bear the separation no more.[5]

'Abdu'l-Bahá built Ḥájí Mullá Mihdí's grave with His own hands. Bahá'u'lláh revealed for him a wondrous Tablet, praising his lofty station and whenever He passed by that grave on His way to 'Akká or to Mazra'ih, He would pause there for a few moments, with one foot on Ḥájí Mullá Mihdí's grave.

The Mansion of Mazra'ih.

Bahjí, the Mansion.

CHAPTER 25

BAHJÍ – THE LOFTY MANSION

MAZRA'IH, though a delightful spot, was too small a house for the needs of Bahá'u'lláh, His family and the increasing numbers of pilgrims arriving in the Holy Land. In 1879, an epidemic disease, probably bubonic plague, swept through the countryside around 'Akká, causing many deaths and a general panic. Many fled the area.

'Udí Khammár, in whose house Bahá'u'lláh had lived when first released from the barracks, was now living in his newly-built mansion at Bahjí. He fell victim to this latest epidemic and died. He was buried by the wall of his mansion and his family fled the area. Soon after his death, 'Abdu'l-Bahá was able to rent the mansion for Bahá'u'lláh and it was later purchased.

Here, in this beautiful and dignified mansion, on which so much wealth and care had been lavished, Bahá'u'lláh was to spend the remaining years of His earthly life. The edict of banishment and of strict and solitary incarceration was never revoked but it was, by this time, simply a dead letter.

Bahá'u'lláh continued, as at Mazra'ih, to spend some time in 'Akká. He frequently visited the homes of His brothers there and from time to time the homes of His followers. He also visited nearby gardens and villages and several times His tent was pitched on a hill near 'Akká where red poppies and anemones flowered in abundance. In 1883 He paid a short visit to Haifa and stayed in a house in the German Templer colony which had been established at the foot of Mount Carmel in the 1860s. The Templers were German Protestants who settled at Haifa in the firm belief that the second coming of Jesus Christ would shortly occur on Mount Carmel. Their first members arrived in 1863 and the colony was established in 1868, the same year in which Bahá'u'lláh reached the Holy Land.

In 1870 'Údí Khammár had placed over the entrance to the mansion of Bahjí an inscription which can be seen there today. It reads: 'Greetings and salutations rest upon this Mansion which increaseth in splendour through the passage of time. Manifold wonders and marvels are found therein, and pens are baffled in attempting to describe them.'[1]

Bahá'u'lláh described Bahjí as 'the lofty mansion' and states, in one Tablet that it was especially built to serve His needs, though 'Údí Khammár, its builder, had no idea for Whom he was building it. In the same Tablet Bahá'u'lláh writes that 'Údí Khammár, in the spiritual world, is assured of the bounties and blessings of God.[2]

Though now residing in this splendid mansion, Bahá'u'lláh continued to live a life of simplicity, avoiding all personal luxury and ostentation. However, He is reported to have stated: 'Sulṭán 'Abdu'l-'Azíz banished Us to this country in the greatest abasement, and since his object was to destroy Us and humble Us, whenever the means of glory and ease presented themselves, We did not reject them.'[3]

Already the prestige of the Bahá'í community was considerable and around this time it rose even higher as the result of a visit that 'Abdu'l-Bahá made to Beirut on the invitation of its Governor, Midḥát Páshá, a former Grand Vizier of the Ottoman Empire. 'Abdu'l-Bahá was received there with great honour and respect.

In 1885, when Bahá'u'lláh's daughter, Furúghíyyih, was married, the Governor of 'Akká and all the high officials of the city attended the wedding feast. In 1887, when Bahá'u'lláh's brother Mírzá Músá died, the notables of 'Akká, together with the Muslim and Christian divines of the city, followed the funeral cortège. During these years, 'Azíz

Páshá, who had been Deputy Governor in Adrianople while Bahá'u'lláh was an exile in that city, twice came to 'Akká from Beirut with the sole intent of visiting Bahá'u'lláh and 'Abdu'l-Bahá.

'Abdu'l-Bahá continued to shield His Father from the pressures of meeting with officials and Bahá'u'lláh seldom granted personal interviews to any but the Bahá'ís. As 'Abdu'l-Bahá writes:

> . . . the doors of majesty and true sovereignty were flung wide open . . . The rulers of Palestine envied His influence and power. Governors and mutiṣarrifs, generals and local officials, would humbly request the honour of attaining His presence – a request to which He seldom acceded.[4]

As the community of believers in Persia and elsewhere steadily expanded, the stream of pilgrims reaching 'Akká increased. Bahá'u'lláh was constantly engaged in revealing Tablets, in answering letters brought to Him and meeting with the pilgrims. A devoted believer in Beirut, Muḥammad Muṣṭafá, provided facilities and assistance for pilgrims reaching and leaving 'Akká. A Bahá'í agency was established in Alexandria to speed up the despatch and distribution of letters going to and from 'Akká. Every year, as he had done since the early days in 'Iráq, Shaykh Salmán arrived from Persia, bearing letters from the believers and every single year, he came, as 'Abdu'l-Bahá writes:

> . . . with the greatest eagerness and love, and then went back again . . . He travelled on foot, as a rule eating nothing but onions and bread; and in all that time, he moved about in such a way that he was never once held up and never once lost a letter or a Tablet. Every letter was safely delivered; every Tablet reached its intended recipient.[5]

The volume of the writings which Bahá'u'lláh revealed during the twenty-four years He spent in the 'Akká area is prodigious. It far exceeds the very considerable volume of those He revealed either in Baghdád or Adrianople. They were poured out, like a mighty river of life-giving water, vitalizing the lives of the pilgrims and of all the believers. It was these writings, together with the pilgrimages undertaken to the presence of Bahá'u'lláh, that enabled the new Faith to grow and develop in Persia, in spite of the relentless persecution.

Refreshed and exhilarated by attaining to the presence of Bahá'u'lláh, the pilgrims set out again to cheer and refresh those who could not travel to 'Akká. They travelled hundreds of miles, often encountering poverty, hardship and hostility, to deepen the believers in the essentials of their Faith. Through the brightness of their words and deeds, they attracted new seekers and, when called upon to do so, they yielded up their lives in His path.

Several other important developments took place during these years. The holy House of the Báb in Shíráz was restored and its custodianship entrusted to the Báb's wife and her sister. In India, five volumes of Bahá'u'lláh's writings, including the *Kitáb-i-Aqdas*, were published. Outposts of believers were established in Samarkand and Bukhárá, a flourishing community developed in 'Ishqábád, in Russian Turkistán and, much nearer to 'Akká, properties were purchased, in the name of the Bahá'í community, on the shores of Lake Galilee.

In the late 1880s, Bahá'u'lláh designated as 'Hands of His Cause' four devoted and knowledgeable believers and charged them with the task of helping the believers to become aware of the laws and principles of the Faith and to exert every effort to carry them out. These appointments, continued by 'Abdu'l-Bahá and Shoghi Effendi, led to the creation of one arm of the Bahá'í administrative order, a system of administration unique in religious history.

In 1890 Bahá'u'lláh paid another visit to Haifa and again stayed in a house in the German Templer colony. During this visit, His tent was pitched on Mount Carmel above what was then the small port of Haifa, just as He had predicted it would be while shut away in the gloomy citadel of 'Akká.

Also in 1890, a brilliant oriental scholar, Professor Edward Granville Browne, a Fellow of Pembroke College, Cambridge, reached 'Akká in the hope of visiting Bahá'u-'lláh. Just a few years earlier, in 1887/8, the young Browne, already fluent in Persian and Arabic, had spent twelve months travelling alone through Persia. There he had encountered many of the believers and had been drawn to investigate the movement further. He arrived in 'Akká on 15 April 1890 and writes of his visit:

> Here did I spend five most memorable days, during which I enjoyed unparalleled and unhoped-for opportunities of holding intercourse with those who are the fountain-heads of that mighty and wondrous spirit, which works with invisible but every-increasing force for the transformation and quickening of a people who slumber in a sleep like unto death. It was, in truth, a strange and moving experience, but one whereof I despair of conveying any save the feeblest impression.[6]

Despite his own feelings of inadequacy, Professor Browne has left a vivid account of his interview with Bahá'u'lláh which took place at Bahjí:

> . . . my conductor paused for a moment while I removed my shoes. Then, with a quick movement of the hand, he withdrew, and, as I passed, replaced the curtain; and I found myself in a large apartment, along the upper end of which ran a low divan, while on the side opposite to the door were placed two or three chairs. Though I dimly suspected whither I was going and whom I was to behold (for no distinct intimation had been given to me), a second or two elapsed ere, with a throb of wonder and awe, I became definitely conscious that the room was not untenanted. In the corner where the divan met the wall sat a wondrous and venerable

figure, crowned with a felt head-dress of the kind called táj by dervishes (but of unusual height and make), round the base of which was wound a small white turban. The face of him on whom I gazed I can never forget, though I cannot describe it. Those piercing eyes seemed to read one's very soul; power and authority sat on that ample brow; while the deep lines on the forehead and face implied an age which the jet-black hair and beard flowing down in indistinguishable luxuriance almost to the waist seemed to belie. No need to ask in whose presence I stood, as I bowed myself before one who is the object of a devotion and love which kings might envy and emperors sigh for in vain!

A mild dignified voice bade me be seated, and then continued: – 'Praise be to God that thou has attained! . . . Thou has come to see a prisoner and an exile . . . We desire but the good of the world and the happiness of the nations; yet they deem us a stirrer up of strife and sedition worthy of bondage and banishment . . . That all nations should become one in faith and all men as brothers; that the bonds of affection and unity between the sons of men should be strengthened; that diversity of religion should cease, and differences of race be annulled – what harm is there in this? . . . Yet so it shall be; these fruitless strifes, these ruinous wars shall pass away, and the "Most Great Peace" shall come . . . Do not you in Europe need this also? Is not this that which Christ foretold? . . . Yet do we see your kings and rulers lavishing their treasures more freely on means for the destruction of the human race than on that which would conduce to the happiness of mankind . . . These strifes and this bloodshed and discord must cease, and all men be as one kindred and one family . . . Let not a man glory in this, that he loves his country; let him rather glory in this, that he loves his kind . . .'

Such, so far as I can recall them, were the words which, besides many others, I heard from Behá. Let those who read them consider well with themselves whether such doctrines merit death and bonds, and whether the world is more likely to gain or lose by their diffusion.[7]

In the spring of 1891 Bahá'u'lláh visited Haifa again and this time His visit lasted for three months. During this visit He instructed 'Abdu'l-Bahá to arrange for the earthly remains of the Báb to be transported from Persia to the Holy Land and pointed out the exact spot on Mount Carmel where they should be laid to rest. It was probably in this year, 1891, that He visited the Cave of Elijah. His tent was certainly pitched near the cave, close to the Carmelite monastery. At this spot Bahá'u'lláh revealed the *Tablet of Carmel* which Shoghi Effendi describes as the Charter for the development of the Bahá'í World Centre. This World Centre is now situated on the slope of Mount Carmel, adjacent to the Shrine of the Báb and facing over the bay of Haifa towards 'Akká.

Up to that time Bahá'u'lláh had not revealed any writings relating to the physical spot where the international centre of His Faith would be located. In the *Tablet of Carmel*, He addresses the mountain itself in these rich and powerful sentences:

> Rejoice, for God hath in this Day established upon thee His throne, hath made thee the dawning-place of His signs and the day spring of the evidences of His Revelation . . . Ere long will God sail His Ark upon thee, and will manifest the people of Bahá who have been mentioned in the Book of Names.[8]

At the time that Bahá'u'lláh walked on the slopes of Mount Carmel the area was a barren and rocky wilderness. The visits that He made to this mountainside and the words He revealed there released the spiritual and material energies that would, over the next century, bring into being the international centre of the Bahá'í world community, where the spiritual and administrative centres of this world-embracing order are now permanently established.

On 19 May 1891 a savage attack was launched against the

Bahá'ís of Yazd, in southern Persia. The accounts of pilgrimages made by the believers and the writings of the Faith which were circulating had aroused the fury of the divines and the ordinary citizens. At the instigation of the mujtahid of Yazd and on the orders of the city's Governor, a grandson of the Sháh, seven Bahá'ís were, in the course of one day, brutally murdered while a frenzied and bloodthirsty crowd cheered on the murderers. The news of the massacre reached Bahá'u'lláh while He was still in Haifa. For nine days all revelation ceased as He grieved for those killed and no one was admitted into His presence. Immediately after those nine days Bahá'u'lláh revealed the stirring Tablet the *Lawḥ-i-Dunyá*, the Tablet of the World:

> Justice is, in this day, bewailing its plight, and Equity groaneth beneath the yoke of oppression. The thick clouds of tyranny have darkened the face of the earth, and enveloped its peoples. Through the movement of Our Pen of glory We have, at the bidding of the omnipotent Ordainer, breathed a new life into every human frame, and instilled into every word a fresh potency. All created things proclaim the evidences of this world-wide regeneration. This is the most great, the most joyful tidings imparted by the Pen of this wronged One to mankind. Wherefore fear ye, O My well-beloved ones?[9]

> Arise for the triumph of My Cause, and, through the power of thine utterance subdue the hearts of men.[10]

> Be as brilliant as the light, and as splendid as the fire that blazed in the Burning Bush. The brightness of the fire of your love will no doubt fuse and unify the contending peoples and kindreds of the earth . . .[11]

CHAPTER 26

'BE NOT DISMAYED, O PEOPLES . . .'

In November 1891 Bahá'u'lláh entered the seventy-fifth year of His earthly life. The years at Mazra'ih and Bahjí had been considerably calmer and more tranquil than those of earlier decades but His physical frame had been severely weakened by earlier events: poison, beating, the prolonged torture of the months spent in the Síyáh-Chál and the two years spent in the Most Great Prison. As His physical strength ebbed, so too did the full flood-tide of His Revelation.

In September of 1891 Bahá'u'lláh intimated to 'Abdu'l-Bahá that He desired to depart from this physical world. In 1886 His beloved wife Navváb had passed away and the following year had seen the loss of Mírzá Músá, His full brother, His most loyal supporter. Bahá'u'lláh never spoke openly to His followers of His physical departure from them but it became evident, from the tone of His remarks and from the urgency with which He seemed to be arranging His affairs, that this event could not be far distant.

In the last year of His life, Bahá'u'lláh revealed His last major work the *Epistle to the Son of the Wolf*. This book is addressed to Shaykh Muḥammad-Taqí, a son of Shaykh Muḥammad-Báqir, the mujtahid of Iṣfáhán who had been responsible for the deaths of the two eminent merchants of the city executed in 1879. Shaykh Muḥammad-Taqí was just as bitterly opposed to the new Faith as was His father and in 1883 had succeeded to his father's position of leading mujtahid in Iṣfáhán.

The *Epistle to the Son of the Wolf*, in which Bahá'u'lláh re-reveals many passages from His earlier works, may be looked upon, in one sense, as an anthology of His own writings. In it He also addresses 'the people of the Bayan', the followers of Mírzá Yaḥyá, quoting extensively from the Báb's own book, the *Bayán*, although, as He clearly states, He had never read it:

> This Wronged One hath been perpetually afflicted, and found no place of safety in which He could peruse either the writings of the Most Exalted One (the Báb) or those of any one else . . . We have, at all times, been busied with the propagation of this Cause. Neither chains nor bonds, stocks nor imprisonment, have succeeded in withholding Us from revealing Our Self . . . We had no other purpose except to edify the souls of men, and to exalt the blessed Word.[1]

On 8 May 1892 Bahá'u'lláh contracted a slight fever which grew worse the next day and then subsided. While He continued to grant interviews to some of the believers, He was still feeling the effects of the fever. Nabíl was admitted to His presence on the third day of His illness:

> On Tuesday this helpless servant was given the honour of an audience with His blessed Person. At noon He summoned me to His presence alone and spoke to me for about half an hour, sometimes seated and sometimes pacing up and down. He vouchsafed unto me His infinite bounties and His exalted utterances reached the acme of perfection.
>
> I wish I had known that this was going to be my last audience with Him . . .[2]

In the following days, Shoghi Effendi recounts:

> His fever returned in a more acute form than before, His general condition grew steadily worse, complications ensued . . .
>
> Six days before He passed away He summoned to His presence, as He lay in bed leaning against one of His sons, the

> entire company of believers, including several pilgrims . . . for what proved to be their last audience with Him. 'I am well pleased with you all,' He gently and affectionately addressed the weeping crowd that gathered about Him. 'Ye have rendered many services, and been very assiduous in your labours . . . May God assist you to remain united. May He aid you to exalt the Cause of the Lord of being.' To the women, including members of His own family, gathered at His bedside, He addressed similar words of encouragement, definitely assuring them that in a document entrusted by Him to the Most Great Branch ['Abdu'l-Bahá] He had commended them all to His care.[3]

Eight hours after sunset, on 29 May 1892, Bahá'u'lláh's spirit left its mortal frame. It was three o'clock in the morning. At once and with all speed a horseman was despatched to carry the news to the Muftí of 'Akká. A cable was sent immediately from 'Akká to the Ottoman Sulṭán 'Abdu'l-Ḥamíd. It began, 'the Sun of Baha has set'.[4]

In 'Akká itself the news was proclaimed from the seven minarets of the mosque:

> God is great.
> He giveth life! He taketh it again!
> He dieth not, but liveth for evermore![5]

This proclamation is only made at the passing of a very greatly honoured, learned and holy man.

From all the mosques throughout Palestine the news was proclaimed and people from every side came to Bahjí to honour Him, to mourn their loss and to pay their respects to the bereaved family. Bahá'u'lláh's body was laid to rest in a room in a house adjacent to the Mansion of Bahjí on the same day in which He left this world. The burial took place shortly after sunset.

Written tributes to Bahá'u'lláh came from Damascus, Aleppo, Beirut and Cairo, while the leading citizens of the immediate neighbourhood came in person. Ṭúbá Khánum relates that:

> Muslim friends, the Muftí, mullás, Governor and officials, Christian priests, Latin and Greek, Druses from from Abú-Sinán, and surrounding villages, and many other friends gathered together in great numbers in honour of the Beloved One.
>
> Marthíyih, songs in His praise, were chanted by poets. Laments and prayers were chanted by Shaykhs. Funeral orations were spoken, describing His wonderful life of self-sacrifice.
>
> Many of the guests encamped under the trees around the Palace of Bahjí, where more than five hundred were entertained for nine days.[6]

Nabíl, overwhelmed with grief, wrote of that agonizing time:

> Methinks, the spiritual commotion set up in the world of dust had caused all the worlds of God to tremble . . . My inner and outer tongue are powerless to portray the condition we were in . . . In the midst of the prevailing confusion a multitude of the inhabitants of 'Akká and of the neighbouring villages, that had thronged the fields surrounding the Mansion, could be seen weeping, beating upon their heads, and crying aloud their grief.[7]

★ ★ ★

The will which Bahá'u'lláh had written, in His own hand, had been kept in 'Akká, in a locked box, for two years. 'Abdu'l-Bahá now sent to 'Akká for this box. On the ninth day after Bahá'u'lláh's passing, in the presence of nine witnesses chosen from His companions and members of His family, the box was unlocked and the seal of the will broken open.

On the afternoon of that same day, in the house where He lay buried, the document was read aloud to His sons and to a large company of the believers.

In this document, which is called the *Kitáb-i-'Ahd*, The Book of the Covenant, Bahá'u'lláh explicitly and unambiguously appoints 'Abdu'l-Bahá as His successor. Referring back to a sentence He had earlier revealed in the *Kitáb-i-Aqdas*, He states:

> The Will of the divine Testator is this: It is incumbent upon the Aghṣán, the Afnán and My kindred to turn, one and all, their faces towards the Most Mighty Branch. Consider that which We have revealed in Our Most Holy Book: 'When the ocean of My presence hath ebbed and the Book of My Revelation is ended, turn your faces toward Him Whom God hath purposed, Who hath branched from this Ancient Root.' The object of this sacred verse is none other except the Most Mighty Branch ('Abdu'l-Bahá). Thus have We graciously revealed unto you our potent Will, and I am verily the Gracious, the All-Powerful.[8]

'Abdu'l-Bahá, now forty-six years old, in obedience to Bahá'u'lláh's explicit instructions, took up the heavy burden of leadership of the Bahá'í community.

NOTE ON SOURCES

THIS account of the life of Bahá'u'lláh is based, in large part, on the following works: *The Dawn-Breakers: Nabíl's Narrative of the Early Days of the Bahá'í Revelation* by Nabíl-i-A'ẓam, *God Passes By*, by Shoghi Effendi, two titles by H.M. Balyuzi, *Bahá'u'lláh, The Word Made Flesh* and *Bahá'u'lláh, The King of Glory*, and the four volumes of *The Revelation of Bahá'u'lláh* by Adib Taherzadeh.

The author wishes also to acknowledge her indebtedness to Hands of the Cause 'Alí-Akbar Furútan and Dr John E. Esslemont, to Lady Blomfield, Dr Moojan Momen and Dr David Ruhe whose works on the history of the Bahá'í Faith are listed in the bibliography, and also to the travellers and authors Gertrude Bell, Freya Stark, Robert Byron and E.B. Soane for their vivid descriptions of some of the places mentioned in this book.

The author's intention has been to provide a clear and straightforward historical account of the life of Bahá'u'lláh. It is her hope that, once this is obtained, her readers will be able to turn with confidence and enthusiasm to the titles listed above.

For those who wish to refer to exact quotations – for example, words spoken by Bahá'u'lláh and various other people – and to the episodes surrounding them, page references are provided.

It is sometimes remarked that very few women appear in the histories of the Middle East of the last century. The reason for this is that there is often no information written down in contemporary records about them. Most chroniclers of the time considered women so insignificant that very little was recorded, or even orally transmitted, about their lives. Thus the reseacher into this period can rarely find more than a cursory mention of the women who were obviously involved in the events of their day.

The Bahá'í Faith recognizes the equality of women and men and sets out the requirements for its establishment as a reality in society. We must now progress quickly towards the day when all people everywhere accept this truth and women are accepted into full partnership with men in all aspects of life. Only then will the true contribution of women to the progress of human civilization be wholly recognized and properly recorded.

LIST OF NAMES

This is a list of the names of those people who appear in the narrative on more than one occasion, in alphabetical order.

'Abdu'l-Bahá	the eldest son of Bahá'u'lláh, He was born on 23 May 1844, the same night on which the Báb declared His mission. He shared in His father's exile and sufferings. Bahá'u'lláh appointed Him as His own successor
Abu'l-Qásim of Hamadán	the companion of Bahá'u'lláh on his journey to Kurdistán, he was murdered by robbers while pursuing his trade in the mountain regions
Aḥmad Big Tawfíq	a governor of 'Akká in the 1870s who became devoted to Bahá'u'lláh
'Alí-Muḥammad, the Báb	the Qá'im, the Promised One. He was born in S͟híráz in 1819, declared His mission in 1844 to prepare the way for 'Him Whom God shall make manifest', and was martyred in Tabríz on 9 July 1850
'Alí Pás͟há	a chief minister at the Ottoman court in the 1860s, it was he, as Grand Vizier, together with Fu'ád Pás͟há, the Minister for Foreign Affairs, who arranged for Bahá'u'lláh's exile to Adrianople

Áqá Ḥusayn-i-Á<u>sh</u>chí	a young believer who served in Bahá'u-'lláh's household from the departure from Ba<u>gh</u>dád onwards. In Adrianople and 'Akká he served as cook
Áqá Ján Big-i-Kaj-Kuláh	a former Turkish artillery officer, he became a staunch supporter of Siyyid Muḥammad and Mírzá Yaḥyá in Adrianople. He was murdered in 'Akká in 1872
Áqá Riḍá	a Bahá'í of <u>Sh</u>íráz, he accompanied Bahá'u'lláh on every stage of His exile and served as His steward
Ásíyih <u>Kh</u>ánum	the first wife of Bahá'u'lláh, mother of 'Abdu'l-Bahá, Bahíyyih <u>Kh</u>ánum and Mírzá Mihdí. Bahá'u'lláh honoured her with the title Navváb. She passed away in 'Akká in 1886
Azíz Pá<u>sh</u>á	Deputy Governor of Adrianople while Bahá'u'lláh was in exile there. He later travelled to 'Akká for the purpose of meeting Bahá'u'lláh and 'Abdu'l-Bahá
Badrí-Ján	a wife of Mírzá Yaḥyá, she became estranged from him but continued to make trouble for the Bahá'ís in 'Akká
Bahá'u'lláh	born Mírzá Ḥusayn 'Alí, He adopted the title 'Bahá'u'lláh' in 1848. This title is first mentioned in the most important work of the Báb, the *Bayán*
Bahíyyih <u>Kh</u>ánum	the eldest daughter of Bahá'u'lláh. She accompanied Him throughout His exile and dedicated her life to serving Him. He bestowed on her the title 'The Greatest Holy Leaf'
Dayyán	a distinguished follower of the Báb, he

	travelled to Baghdád and was there murdered on the orders of Mírzá Yaḥyá
Ḥájí Mírzá Aḥmad	a Bábí from Káshán, he became a follower of Mírzá Yaḥyá
Ḥájí Mírzá Áqásí	Grand Vizier to Muḥammad Sháh. He had been the Sháh's religious tutor. He fell from power in 1848 and died in 1849
Ḥájí Mírzá Ḥusayn Khán	the Persian Ambassador in Constantinople during the 1860s. He was, in large part, responsible for Bahá'u'lláh's exile to Adrianople
Ḥujjat – Mullá Muḥammad-'Alí	a learned and outspoken religious leader of Zanján who became a Bábí. He was martyred in Zanján in 1850
Ilyás 'Abbúd	a prominent citizen of 'Akká, a relative of 'Udí Khammár, at first hostile to Bahá'u'lláh, he later became devoted to Him. Bahá'u'lláh lived for some years in his house in 'Akká
Khadíjih Khánum	mother of Bahá'u'lláh, a noblewoman of Yálrúd, in Núr, the second wife of Mírzá 'Abbás-i-Núrí (Mírzá Buzurg)
Lt. Col Sheil	British Minister in Ṭihrán during the 1850s. His despatches and the letters of his wife, Lady Sheil, are drawn on in this narrative
Mírzá 'Abbás-i-Núrí	also known as Mírzá Buzurg, the Vizier, father of Bahá'u'lláh, a distinguished nobleman of the region of Núr and a minister at the court of Fatḥ-'Alí Sháh. He passed away in 1839
Mírzá Áqá Ján	a Bábí from Káshán, he recognized Bahá'u'lláh's station in Baghdád and

	served as Bahá'u'lláh's amanuensis for many years
Mírzá Áqá Khán-i-Núrí	a distant relative of Bahá'u'lláh, he became Grand Vizier to Náṣiri'd-Dín Sháh in 1851. He fell from power in 1858
Mírzá Buzurg	father of Bahá'u'lláh (also known as Mírzá 'Abbás-i-Núrí)
Mírzá Buzurg Khán	he was made Persian consul-general in Baghdád in 1860 and schemed to have Bahá'u'lláh removed from the city and also tried to have Him assassinated
Mírzá Mihdí	a son of Bahá'u'lláh, he was too young and delicate to share the first journey of exile but joined the exiles in Baghdád and devoted his life to the service of Bahá'u'lláh. He died after falling through an open skylight in the Most Great Prison in 'Akká in 1870
Mírzá Muḥammad-Qulí	a half-brother of Bahá'u'lláh and His loyal follower. He shared in all Bahá'u'lláh's journeys of exile and suffering
Mírzá Músá	brother of Bahá'u'lláh, he accepted the Báb's message in 1844. He accompanied Bahá'u'lláh on His journeys of exile and was throughout His staunch supporter and most loyal companion. He died in 'Akká in 1887
Mírzá Riḍá-Qulí	a brother-in-law of Mírzá Yaḥyá, he was also his follower and was murdered in 'Akká in 1872
Mírzá Taqí Khán	Grand Vizier to Náṣiri'd-Dín Sháh. He was ousted from power in 1850 and murdered in 1851
Mírzá Yaḥyá	a young half-brother of Bahá'u'lláh.

	While the Báb was imprisoned, he was appointed as official nominee of the Báb until such time as 'He Whom God shall make manifest' would appear. He was given the title 'Ṣubḥ-i-Azal' (Morn of Eternity). He never acknowledged Bahá'u'lláh's mission but sought leadership on his own behalf. He died on the island of Cyprus in 1912
Mullá Ḥusayn-i-Bushrú'í	a student of Siyyid Káẓim, the first to search for the Promised One and the first to find Him. He was martyred in 1849 at Shaykh Ṭabarsí
Mullá Shaykh-'Alí of Khurásán	sometimes called 'Aẓím, he was a Bábí and the ringleader of a very small group of Bábís who plotted to assassinate the Sháh as they blamed him for the death of the Báb
Munírih Khánum	a Bahá'í from Shíráz, she travelled to the Most Great Prison and there became the wife of 'Abdu'l-Bahá
Nabíl-i-A'ẓam	Mullá Muḥammad-i-Zarandí, a Bahá'í who compiled *The Dawn-Breakers*, an account of the early days of the Bahá'í Revelation. He drowned himself in the sea shortly after the passing of Bahá'u-'lláh
Namíq Páshá	governor of Baghdád when Bahá'u'lláh was invited to Constantinople, he did all that was possible to ease the difficulties of the exiles' journey
Prince Dolgorouki	the Russian minister at the court of the Sháh in the 1850s, he played a leading role in preventing the execution of

	Bahá'u'lláh and in arranging for His release from the Síyáh-Chál
Quddús	Mullá Muḥammad-'Alíy-i-Bárfurúshí, the youngest in years and foremost in rank of the Báb's first disciples, the Letters of Living. He was martyryed in Bárfurúsh in 1849
Shamsí Big	the Ottoman official given the task of caring for Bahá'u'lláh, His family and companions while they were in Constantinople
Shaykh 'Abdu'l-Ḥusayn	a Shí'ih priest resident in Karbilá who schemed to destroy Bahá'u'lláh's good name in the city
Shaykh Aḥmad-i-Aḥsá'í	a Persian religious teacher who first foretold the coming of the Báb
Shaykh Ḥasan-i-Zunúzí	a Bábí sent by the Báb to live in Karbilá where he recognized Bahá'u'lláh as 'He Whom God shall make manifest' before Bahá'u'lláh declared His mission
Shaykh Salmán	the courier of Bahá'u'lláh, he carried letters from Persia to Bahá'u'lláh and back, every year during Bahá'u'lláh's exile
Siyyid Ḥasan and Siyyid Ḥusayn-i-Yazdí	two Bábí brothers whom the Báb chose to accompany Him in Adharbáyján. Siyyid Ḥusayn was martyred in Ṭihrán in 1852
Siyyid Kázim-i-Rashtí	an outstanding disciple of Shaykh Aḥmad, whom Shaykh Aḥmad appointed as his successor
Siyyid Muḥammad	a Bábí from Iṣfáhán, he was jealous of Bahá'u'lláh's prestige. He schemed, with Mírzá Yaḥyá, to destroy Bahá'u-

	'lláh's authority. He was murdered in 'Akká in 1872
Sulaymán Khán	a prominent Bábí who arranged for the rescue of the remains of the bodies of the Báb and His companion Anís from Tabríz. He was martyred in Ṭihrán in 1852
Ṭáhirih	the only woman amongst the Letters of the Living, the Báb's first disciples. She was martyred in Ṭihrán in 1852
'Údí Khammár	a prominent citizen of 'Akká, Bahá'u-'lláh rented his town house on His release from the Most Great Prison. Later He rented and then bought the mansion which 'Údí Khammár had built at Bahjí
Vaḥíd	Siyyid Yaḥyáy-i-Darabí, an outstanding religious teacher sent to interview the Báb by Muḥammad Sháh. He became a Bábí and was martyred in Nayríz in 1850

SOME PERSIAN AND ARABIC TERMS

Afnán (Twigs)	title given to the descendants of the two brothers of the Báb's wife and of the Báb's maternal uncles
Aghṣán (Branches)	the family of Bahá'u'lláh, particularly His sons and His descendants
Amír	a title of respect given to someone in authority; it can mean lord, prince, governor or commander
Amír-i-Nizám	commander in chief
Áqá	mister
Caliph, Caliphate	in Sunní Islám, a successor of Muḥammad as head of the Faith and the institution created around him
Dervish (Beggar)	a travelling religious mendicant
Ḥadíth (Tradition)	in Islám, oral traditions about things Muḥammad said or did
Ḥájí	a title which is given to any Muslim who has made the pilgrimage to Mecca
Imám	the title given to the twelve Shí'ih successors of the Prophet Muḥammad. It is also given to some important Muslim religious leaders
Imám-Jum'ih	a title given to the most important religious leader in a town or city. He is the chief of all the mullás (religious leaders) in that place

Jamádí	Muslim month
Kalántar	a title meaning 'mayor' or leading civic official in any town or city
Kashkúl	alms bowl carried by a dervish
Muftí	in Sunní Islám, a religious lawyer who provides legal opinions on points of Islamic law
Mujtahid	a doctor of Muslim law
Mullá	a title given to a Muslim religious leader. It can also also mean a judge or theologian
mutiṣarrif	governor of a town
Navváb	a title of honour meaning 'highness'
Naw-Rúz	the traditional Persian New Year, celebrated also by Bahá'ís
Páshá	title given to high-ranking officers
Qá'im	He Who ariseth, the Messenger of God awaited by the Shí'ih Muslims. The Báb claimed to be the Qá'im
Rajab	Muslim month
Sháh	King
Shaykh	a title of respect given to an elder, a wise old man or a man in authority, a professor and a superior of a dervish order
Shaykhí	a follower of Shaykh Aḥmad and Siyyid Káẓim; those of the Shaykhís who did not recognize the Báb continued as a sect of Islám
Shí'ih Islám	one of the two major branches of Islám, Shí'ihs believe that Muḥammad appointed 'Alí to be His successor. Considered by Bahá'u'lláh as followers of the true Islám
Sulṭán	King

Sunní Islám	the main sect of Islám which accepts the caliphs as the successors to Muḥammad
Súrih	a chapter of the Holy Qur'án
'Ulamá	learned clergymen
Vizier	a high executive officer of state, a minister or councillor

N.B. The English noun 'divine' is used interchangeably with 'clergy'

QÁJÁR AND OTTOMAN RULERS

Qájár Rulers of Persia during the Life of Bahá'u'lláh

Fatḥ-'Alí Sháh, 1798–1834
Muḥammad Sháh, 1835–48
Náṣiri'd-Dín Sháh 1848–96

Ottoman Rulers during the Life of Bahá'u'lláh

Sulṭán 'Abdu'l-Majíd, 1839–61
Sulṭán 'Abdu'l-'Azíz, 1861–76
Sulṭán Murád V, 1876
Sulṭán 'Abdu'l-Ḥamíd, 1876–1909

A FEW DATES

1817	Birth of Bahá'u'lláh in Ṭihrán
1819	Birth of the Báb in S͟híráz
1844	23 May – the Báb declares His mission to Mullá Ḥusayn
	August – Mullá Ḥusayn reaches Ṭihrán, Bahá'u'lláh accepts the Báb's message
1848	Bahá'u'lláh is bastinadoed at Ámul
1850	9 July – martyrdom of the Báb
1851	June – Bahá'u'lláh travels to 'Iráq
1852	April/May – Bahá'u'lláh returns to Ṭihrán
	15 August – assassination attempt on the life of the S͟háh.
	August-December – Bahá'u'lláh is imprisoned in the Síyáh-C͟hál
1853	12 January – Bahá'u'lláh is exiled from Ṭihrán
	8 April – Bahá'u'lláh reaches Bag͟hdád
1854	10 April – Bahá'u'lláh leaves Bag͟hdád for Kurdistán
1856	19 March – Bahá'u'lláh returns to Bag͟hdád
1863	22 April – Bahá'u'lláh declares His mission in the Garden of Riḍván
	16 August – Bahá'u'lláh arrives at Constantinople
	1–12 December – the exiles travel to Adrianople
1868	12–31 August – Bahá'u'lláh travels to 'Akká
1870	October – Bahá'u'lláh leaves the Most Great Prison

1873	Bahá'u'lláh reveals the *Kitáb-i-Aqdas*
1877	June – Bahá'u'lláh moves out of 'Akká to Mazra'ih
1879	September – Bahá'u'lláh moves to Bahjí
1892	29 May – ascension of Bahá'u'lláh

BIBLIOGRAPHY

'Abdu'l-Bahá. *Memorials of the Faithful*. Translated and annotated by Marzieh Gail. Wilmette, Illinois: Bahá'í Publishing Trust, 1971.

—— *Selections from the Writings of 'Abdu'l-Bahá*. Translated by a Committee at the Bahá'í World Centre and by Marzieh Gail. Haifa: Bahá'í World Centre, 1978.

Bahá'í Prayers. Wilmette, Illinois: Bahá'í Publishing Trust, 1982.

Bahá'u'lláh. *Epistle to the Son of the Wolf*. Wilmette, Illinois: Bahá'í Publishing Trust, 1962.

—— *Gleanings from the Writings of Bahá'u'lláh*. Translated by Shoghi Effendi. Wilmette, Illinois: Bahá'í Publishing Trust, 1963.

—— *Kitáb-i-Íqán: The Book of Certitude*. Wilmette, Illinois: Bahá'í Publishing Trust, 1960.

—— *The Proclamation of Bahá'u'lláh*. Haifa: Bahá'í World Centre, 1967.

—— *Tablets of Bahá'u'lláh revealed after the Kitáb-i-Aqdas*. Compiled by the Research Department of the Universal House of Justice and translated by Habib Taherzadeh with the assistance of a Committee at the Bahá'í World Centre. Haifa: Bahá'í World Centre, 1978.

Balyuzi, H.M. *Bahá'u'lláh, The Word Made Flesh*. Oxford: George Ronald, 1963.

—— *Bahá'u'lláh, The King of Glory*. Oxford: George Ronald, 1980.

Bell, Gertrude. *Persian Pictures*. London: Jonathan Cape, 1928.

Blomfield, Lady (Sitarih Khanum), *The Chosen Highway*. Wilmette, Illinois: Bahá'í Publishing Trust, 1967.

Byron, Robert. *The Road to Oxiana*. London: Picador, Pan, 1981.

Esslemont, John E. *Bahá'u'lláh and the New Era*. London: Bahá'í Publishing Trust, 1923, rev. 4th edn., 1974.

Furútan, Ali-Akbar. *Stories of Bahá'u'lláh*. Oxford: George Ronald, 1986.

Gail, Marzieh. *The Sheltering Branch*. Oxford: George Ronald, 1959.

Momen, Moojan. *The Babí and Bahá'í Religions, 1844–1944: Some Contemporary Western Accounts*. Oxford: George Ronald, 1981.

Nabíl-i-A'ẓam. *The Dawn-Breakers: Nabíl's Narrative of the Early Days of the Bahá'í Revelation*. Wilmette, Illinois: Bahá'í Publishing Trust, 1932.

Ruhe, David. *Door of Hope: A Century of the Bahá'í Faith in the Holy Land*. Oxford: George Ronald, 1983.

Shoghi Effendi. *God Passes By*. Wilmette, Illinois: Bahá'í Publishing Trust, 1944.

—— *The Promised Day is Come*. Wilmette, Illinois: Bahá'í Publishing Trust, 1961.

Soane, E.B. *To Mesopotamia and Kurdistan in Disguise*. London: John Murray, 1912.

Stark, Freya. *Baghdád Sketches*. London: John Murray, 1937.

Synopsis and Codification of The Kitáb-i-Aqdas, the Most Holy Book of Bahá'u'lláh, A. Haifa: Bahá'í World Centre, 1973.

Taherzadeh, Adib. *The Revelation of Bahá'u'lláh*. vols. 1–4. Oxford: George Ronald, 1974–87.

REFERENCES

1. The Báb cited in *God Passes By*, p. 30.
2. ibid. pp. 30–1.

Preface

1. Gail, *Sheltering Branch*, p. 11.
2. The Báb cited in *God Passes By*, pp. 30–1.

Chapter 1: Early Years

1. Furútan, *Stories of Bahá'u'lláh*, p. 2.
2. Bahá'u'lláh, *Epistle*, p. 39.
3. Byron, *Road to Oxiana*, p. 193.
4. Nabíl, *Dawn-Breakers*, p. 111.
5. ibid. pp. 111–12.
6. ibid. p. 86.
7. ibid. p. 107.

Chapter 2: An Exemplary Disciple

1. Nabíl, *Dawn-Breakers*, pp. 92–4.
2. ibid. p. 113.
3. ibid. p. 116.
4. ibid. p. 127.
5. ibid. pp. 117–18.
6. ibid. pp. 228–9.
7. ibid. p. 299.

Chapter 3: A Darkening Land

1. Nabíl, *Dawn-Breakers*, pp. 315–16.

2. Shoghi Effendi, *God Passes By*, p. 81.
3. Nabíl, *Dawn-Breakers*, pp. 461–2.
4. Momen, *Bábí and Bahá'í Religions*, p. 115.

Chapter 4: A Sombre Episode

1. Nabíl, *Dawn-Breakers*, pp. 554–5.
2. ibid. p. 556.
3. ibid. p. 558.

Chapter 5: The Promised Ḥusayn

1. Balyuzi, *King of Glory*, p. 66.
2. Nabíl, *Dawn-Breakers*, p. 30.
3. ibid. pp. 31–2.
4. ibid. p. 32.
5. ibid. p. 33.

Chapter 6: Calamity

1. Momen, *Bábí and Bahá'í Religions*, p. 137.
2. ibid. p. 131.
3. Nabíl, *Dawn-Breakers*, p. 602.
4. ibid. pp. 607–8.
5. Blomfield, *Chosen Highway*, pp. 40–1.

Chapter 7: A Dark and Dreadful Hour

1. Bahá'u'lláh, *Epistle*, pp. 20–1.
2. ibid. p. 77.
3. Shoghi Effendi, *God Passes By*, p. 75.
4. Momen, *Bábí and Bahá'í Religions*, p. 144.
5. Nabíl, *Dawn-Breakers*, pp. 631–2.
6. Momen, *Bábí and Bahá'í Religions*, pp. 135–6.
7. Nabíl, *Dawn-Breakers*, pp. 632–3.
8. Momen, *Bábí and Bahá'í Religions*, pp. 133–4.
9. ibid. p. 134.
10. ibid. p. 138.
11. Shoghi Effendi, *God Passes By*, p. 64.

12. Momen, *Bábí and Bahá'í Religions*, p. 145.
13. Nabíl, *Dawn-Breakers*, p. 634.

Chapter 8: In the Holy and Shining City

1. Bahá'u'lláh, *Epistle*, p. 21.
2. Shoghi Effendi, *God Passes By*, pp. 101–2.
3. ibid. p. 102.
4. Bahá'u'lláh, *Epistle*, p. 22.
5. Bahá'u'lláh, *Gleanings*, p. 121.
6. ibid. p. 110.
7. Nabíl, *Dawn-Breakers*, p. 648.
8. ibid. p. 649.
9. Blomfield, *Chosen Highway*, p. 45.
10. Momen, *Bábí and Bahá'í Religions*, p. 123.
11. Shoghi Effendi, *God Passes By*, p. 113.

Chapter 9: To Baghdád

1. Stark, *Baghdád Sketches*, p. 62.
2. ibid. p. 18.

Chapter 10: Woes at Their Blackest

1. Bahá'u'lláh, *Epistle*, p. 21.
2. Balyuzi, *King of Glory*, pp. 109–11.
3. Bahá'u'lláh cited in *God Passes By*, p. 118.
4. ibid. p. 119.
5. Shoghi Effendi, *God Passes By*, p. 119.
6. Bahá'u'lláh cited in ibid. p. 119.

Chapter 11: In the Wilderness

1. Bahá'u'lláh cited in *God Passes By*, p. 120.
2. ibid. p. 119.
3. Bahá'u'lláh, *Íqán*, p. 251.
4. ibid. pp. 250–1.
5. Bahá'u'lláh, *Bahá'í Prayers*, p. 142.
6. Shoghi Effendi, *God Passes By*, p. 123.

7. 'Abdu'l-Bahá cited in ibid. p. 124.
8. Bahá'u'lláh cited in ibid.
9. ibid. p. 126.
10. ibid.

Chapter 12: A Rising Splendour

1. Blomfield, *Chosen Highway*, pp. 53–4.
2. Bahá'u'lláh cited in *God Passes By*, p. 125.
3. Bahá'u'lláh, *Íqán*, p. 252.
4. Shoghi Effendi, *God Passes By*, pp. 132–3.
5. ibid. p. 135.
6. Nabíl cited in *God Passes By*, p. 134.
7. ibid. p. 137.
8. Furútan, *Stories of Bahá'u'lláh*, p. 26.
9. Bahá'u'lláh cited in *God Passes By*, p. 137.
10. ibid.
11. ibid. p. 133.
12. Shoghi Effendi, *God Passes By*, p. 140.
13. ibid. p. 139.
14. ibid. p. 138.
15. ibid.
16. Bahá'u'lláh cited in *King of Glory*, p. 148.
17. Balyuzi, *King of Glory*, p. 143.
18. Bahá'u'lláh cited in *God Passes By*, p. 144.
19. ibid.
20. Bahá'u'lláh cited in *King of Glory*, p. 148.
21. Bahá'u'lláh cited in *God Passes By*, p. 149.

Chapter 13: The Divine Springtime

1. Bahá'u'lláh, *Gleanings*, pp. 33–4.
2. Nabíl cited in *God Passes By*, p. 153.
3. ibid.
4. Bahá'u'lláh cited in *King of Glory*, pp. 174–5.
5. Nabíl cited in *God Passes By*, p. 155.

Chapter 14: A Triumphal Progress

1. Bahá'u'lláh cited in *King of Glory*, p. 183.
2. Nabíl cited in *God Passes By*, p. 156.
3. Soane, *To Mesopotamia*, p. 82.
4. Nabíl cited in *God Passes By*, pp. 156–7.

Chapter 15: Hurried from Land to Land

1. Bahá'u'lláh cited in *Chosen Highway*, p. 59.
2. Bahá'u'lláh, *Gleanings*, pp. 126–7.
3. Shoghi Effendi, *God Passes By*, p. 160.
4. Bahá'u'lláh cited in ibid.
5. Balyuzi, *King of Glory*, p. 202.
6. Bahá'u'lláh cited in ibid. p. 203.
7. Bahá'u'lláh cited in *God Passes By*, p. 160.
8. Nabíl cited in ibid. p. 161.
9. ibid.

Chapter 16: Days of Stress

1. Bahá'u'lláh cited in *God Passes By*, p. 161.
2. Shoghi Effendi, *God Passes By*, p. 167.
3. Bahá'u'lláh cited in *King of Glory*, p. 233.
4. Bahá'u'lláh cited in *God Passes By*, pp. 168–9.
5. Shoghi Effendi, *God Passes By*, pp. 163–4.

Chapter 17: Land of Mystery

1. Bahá'u'lláh cited in *God Passes By*, p. 169.
2. ibid.
3. ibid.
4. Nabíl cited in ibid. p. 171.
5. Bahá'u'lláh cited in ibid.
6. Bahá'u'lláh, *Gleanings*, pp. 250–1.

Chapter 18: To the Desolate City

1. Bahá'u'lláh cited in *God Passes By*, pp. 179–80.
2. Bahá'u'lláh cited in *Promised Day is Come*, p. 62.

3. Bahá'u'lláh cited in *God Passes By*, p. 181.
4. ibid. p. 182.
5. ibid.

Chapter 19: The Most Great Prison

1. Bahá'u'lláh cited in *God Passes By*, p. 184.
2. ibid. p. 185.
3. Bahá'u'lláh cited in *Dawn-Breakers*, p. 585.

Chapter 20: Close Confinement

1. Bahá'u'lláh cited in *King of Glory*, p. 360.
2. Bahá'u'lláh, *Proclamation*, p. 17.
3. ibid. pp. 27–8.
4. ibid. p. 33.
5. ibid. p. 34.
6. ibid. p. 83.
7. Nabíl cited in *King of Glory*, p. 294.
8. Taherzadeh, *Revelation 3*, p. 183.
9. ibid. pp. 183–4.
10. ibid. p. 186.
11. Balyuzi, *King of Glory*, p. 307.

Chapter 21: The Prison Doors Open

1. Shoghi Effendi, *God Passes By*, p. 186.
2. Taherzadeh, *Revelation 3*, p. 207.
3. Balyuzi, *King of Glory*, pp. 311–12.
4. ibid. p. 311.
5. Bahá'u'lláh cited in *Revelation 3*, p. 213.
6. ibid. p. 210.
7. Bahíyyih Khánum cited in *Chosen Highway*, p. 68.

Chapter 22: A Fresh Danger

1. Bahá'u'lláh, *Fire Tablet*, in *Bahá'í Prayers*, pp. 215–18.
2. Balyuzi, *King of Glory*, p. 326.
3. Shoghi Effendi, *God Passes By*, pp. 190–1.

4. Bahá'u'lláh cited in ibid. pp. 189–90.

Chapter 23: The Turning Tide

1. Bahá'u'lláh cited in *God Passes By*, p. 190.
2. 'Abdu'l-Bahá, *Selections*, p. 263.
3. Bahá'u'lláh cited in *God Passes By*, p. 216.
4. Shoghi Effendi, *God Passes By*, p. 213.
5. ibid. p. 212.
6. Bahá'u'lláh cited in ibid.
7. Shoghi Effendi, *God Passes By*, p. 213.
8. The Universal House of Justice cited in *Revelation 3*, p. 283.
9. Bahá'u'lláh, *Synopsis and Codification*, pp. 11–12.
10. Taherzadeh, *Revelation 3*, p. 403.
11. Shoghi Effendi, *God Passes By*, p. 192.
12. Bahá'u'lláh cited in *New Era*, p. 33.
13. 'Abdu'l-Bahá cited in ibid., pp. 34–5.

Chapter 24: Mazra'ih – A Place of Freedom

1. Taherzadeh, *Relevation 4*, p. 5.
2. Ṭúbá Khánum cited in *Chosen Highway*, p. 97.
3. Shoghi Effendi, *God Passes By*, p. 197.
4. Bahá'u'lláh cited in ibid.
5. 'Abdu'l-Bahá, *Memorials*, pp. 85–6.

Chapter 25: Bahjí – The Lofty Mansion

1. Ruhe, *Door*, p. 107.
2. Taherzadeh, *Revelation 4*, p. 104.
3. Shoghi Effendi, *God Passes By*, p. 195.
4. 'Abdu'l-Bahá cited in ibid. p. 193.
5. 'Abdu'l-Bahá, *Memorials*, p. 15.
6. Browne cited in *God Passes By*, p. 194.
7. Balyuzi, *King of Glory*, pp. 371–3.
8. Bahá'u'lláh, *Gleanings*, pp. 15–16.
9. ibid. pp. 92–3.

10. ibid. p. 92.
11. ibid. p. 96.

Chapter 26: 'Be Not Dismayed, O Peoples . . .'

1. Bahá'u'lláh, *Epistle*, p. 166.
2. Nabíl cited in *Revelation 4*, pp. 414–15.
3. Shoghi Effendi, *God Passes By*, pp. 221–2.
4. ibid. p. 222.
5. Blomfield, *Chosen Highway*, p. 106.
6. Ṭúbá Kh̲ánum cited in ibid. pp. 106–7.
7. Nabíl cited in *God Passes By*, p. 222.
8. Bahá'u'lláh, *Tablets*, pp. 221–2.